The Complete Beginner's Guide to Horseback Riding

The Complete Beginner's Guide: Handball & Hockey

The Complete Beginner's Guide to
HORSEBACK RIDING

GIL PAUST

Doubleday & Company, Inc., Garden City, New York   1977

Library of Congress Cataloging in Publication Data

Paust, Gil.
The complete beginner's guide to horseback riding.

SUMMARY: A complete guide to riding, selecting, and
caring for horses.
1. Horses—Juvenile literature. 2. Horsemanship—
Juvenile literature. [1. Horses. 2. Horsemanship] I. Title.
SF302.P38   798'.23
ISBN: 0-385-01747-2 Trade
0-385-03347-8 Prebound
Library of Congress Catalog Card Number 76–42380

9 8 7 6 5 4 3 2

To my wife, Anne, who is devoted to all animals, especially horses, and who took most of the photos appearing on these pages.

Acknowledgments

My sincere thanks to the following for their assistance: American Connemara Pony Society; American Paint Horse Association; American Quarter Horse Association; American Saddle Horse Breeders Association; Black Hills Trail Ride, Inc., Rapid City, South Dakota; Champion Boot Company, El Paso, Texas; Churchill Downs, Inc.; Eiser's, Inc., a saddlery in Hillside, New Jersey; Kauffman & Sons, equestrian supplies in New York City; Lee Western Apparel; Meredith Manor, Waverly, West Virginia, a complete "college" for beginning and advanced riders; Peter Winants, editor of *The Chronicle of the Horse* magazine; Tennessee Walking Horse Breeders' and Exhibitors' Association; Tex Tan Western Leather Company; Trail Riders of the Wilderness, Mary Ellen Walsh, director; United States Forest Service Photo Library; United States Pony Clubs, Inc.; Arnold Weiner of The Village Saddlery, Larchmont, New York; Wrangler Western Wear; and special thanks to Robert Helbock of the Kentucky Stables in Harrison, New York, and to my very photogenic models eighteen-year-old Pat Cuccia and eight-year-old Sky Budin.

Contents

SECTION I
All About Horses

Eohippus, *ancient ancestor of the modern horse.*

1. Sixty Million Years of Horses

During the Eocene Period of geological history, called the Dawn Age of mammals—about 58 million years before the first man appeared on earth—a strange little animal skulked through the steaming swamps that covered prehistoric North America. Its fossils reveal it was only about ten inches high, almost hairless, had the sturdy hindquarters of a jack rabbit, and an elongated head with an arched sheeplike nose and short ears. Its short, soft teeth indicate it was a browsing type of herbivore, feeding on swamp plants and ferns. It had stubby legs, each hind foot with three toes and each front foot with four toes, probably webbed. More impressive monsters stalked that ancient world, their huge skeletons on display in museums, but none is more worthy of our appreciation and respect than this tiny creature. It was *Eohippus*, and it survived the ages to become today's tall and stately horse.

Little is known of its origin except that its species must have been developing during the preceding Age of Reptiles when egg-laying dinosaurs and flying dragons dominated the earth. Most significant is the fact that it was one of the first mammals. A mystery that has long baffled paleontologists is the creation of this entirely different life form—the mammal—in a world of egg-layers. Also, the relatively sudden extinction of the giant reptiles which previously had survived for 150 million years.

Traces of similar primitive horses have been found throughout the world except Australia, but all of them eventually became extinct. Only in North America did the species adapt successfully to the environmental changes caused by the shifting and aging face of the earth, and the story of its survival is considered one of the simplest and clearest examples of the evolutionary process.

As the Eocene Period progressed through millions of years, the earth's climate gradually became drier and more temperate. The swamps slowly drained and were replaced by forests; the low plants, upon which the primitive horse depended for food, began to disappear. To survive, it grew larger. Its legs and neck lengthened so it could browse on the overhead leaves and tree sprouts. And since it could no longer avoid predators by hiding in the ground foliage, and since it had no claws, horns, or fangs with which to defend itself, it had to depend upon outdistancing its enemies. Its gait changed from a rabbitlike hop to a leg-swinging run; it had begun to develop into one of the fleetest animals in the world.

At the end of the Oligocene Period, 30 million years later, it resembled today's deer in size and appearance, except for its long head and tail and short bristling mane. It was still small, however, compared to some of the mammals that had also developed in North America at that time, one of which was a rhinoceros, fourteen feet high at the shoulder!

During the Miocene and Pliocene periods, which covered the next 20 million years, the horse changed even more dramatically. It had to develop new feeding habits as the forests were replaced by open plains and grasslands and the tree-browse disappeared. It became a grazer. And this necessitated an entirely new set of teeth because the abrasive minerals in the grass soon wore down the soft teeth that had been adequate for browsing. These were replaced by twenty-four hard-enameled and long-rooted molars which, in today's horse, never stop growing during its lifetime. It also had twelve nippers, or incisors, in front for cutting the grass. And the horse's neck became even longer so it could reach the grass more easily.

If speed had been necessary for escape from its enemies in the forests, it was even more vital in the open plains. The horse's toed feet, however, although well adapted to support and traction in the soft earth of the swamp and early forests, handicapped the heavier animal which had to race over long distances on hard ground. Even in the Eocene Period its feet had begun to change. The four-toed feet became three-toed, then a center toe of each foot grew progressively larger and the side toes smaller until finally there remained only one large toe—the hoof. The unborn embryo of today's horse has the toed feet of its ancient ancestor. The tapir of Southern Asia and South America, a distant relative of the horse with a piglike body and a short trunk for a nose, still has four toes on its front feet and three on its hind feet. By the beginning of the Pleistocene Period, which began about one million years ago, the horse resembled a modern pony. Called *Equus*, it has changed little and is the one from which all modern types have developed. But there was still another interesting chapter in the story of the early horse.

Throughout early history, a land bridge connected Alaska

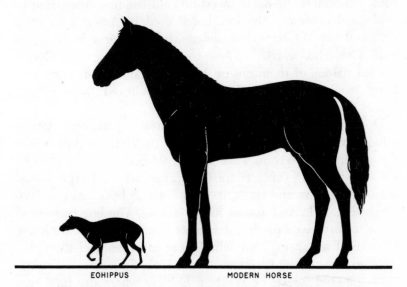

EOHIPPUS   MODERN HORSE

Today's horse compared to the one-foot-high Eohippus.

and Siberia, and it was a migratory route for animals. It was
the way the camel, which originated in North America, found
its way to Asia and Africa. More important, *Equus* also used it
to spread through Asia, Africa, and Europe, continents on
which their own primitive horses had become extinct. If this
migration had not occurred, horses would be unknown in the
modern world because a number of factors combined to exter-
minate them in the Western Hemisphere, and only those that
had moved to these other continents survived.

During the Ice Age, which lasted many thousands of years
and ended in approximately 15,000 B.C., great glaciers moved
down from the Arctic four times, destroying most .of North
America's wildlife. Some horses fled to South America, crossing
the Isthmus of Panama, a land bridge that had formed two million years ago. Others found safety in Central America. But all
survivors eventually disappeared. Famine and an unknown
plague are the generally suspected causes. Some scientists believe they were exterminated by nomadic Stone Age hunters,
ancestors of the Indians, who came from Asia across the
Alaska-Siberia bridge and settled in the Americas. But the Ice
Age was less severe in Europe and Asia, and apparently on
these continents the horse faced no catastrophes. According to
geological evidence, the last horse died in America in 7000
B.C., and the Western Hemisphere did not see a horse again
until Columbus carried a few to Haiti in 1494, and Cortez
landed sixteen of them on the Mexican mainland in 1519, cre-
ating panic among the Indians who believed them savage
beasts that ate only human flesh.

During the horse's existence in Europe, Asia, and Africa,
minor revolutionary changes occurred. In Northern Asia where
the climate and terrain were severe, its body became chunky
with a large lung capacity for endurance, its head grew larger
with strong jaws and teeth, its coat became heavy to conserve
body heat. It looked almost like a jackass. The last truly wild
horse to survive on earth, it has been named *Przewalski's* horse
after the Russian explorer who in the nineteenth century discovered a few living specimens in the Gobi Desert.

In the cold forests of Western Europe where the food was
more abundant and the terrain more level, the horse grew

huge and powerful, and it slowed to a plodding animal rather than a runner. It has been named *Equus robustus* because of its great size and strength. In the milder but mountainous regions of Southern Europe it grew to resemble more nearly the horse as it is commonly known today, and as will be shown later, the Spanish version became one of the ancestors of the American mustang. It is generally referred to as the *Tarpan*. Some authorities claim that the Spanish horse also developed the gait called pacing, a lateral leg movement.

The most important type, however, because it has had the most influence on the development of the modern horse, is one called simply the *Arab* or *Arabian*, from the Mediterranean desert country. Most authorities have assumed that the Arabian is a refinement of the Tarpan, probably introduced to the area by the invading Hyksos armies in 1700 B.C. They have based their beliefs on the lack of fossils to prove the existence of ancient horses in the region, but traces might have been obliterated by the harsh desert sun, sand, and wind. Recent finds in

The Tarpan, *a wild horse that once roamed southern Europe.*

Southern Asia and Lybia, including drawings, show that an Oriental type of horse probably did exist, and it was the ancestor of the Arabian. Geologists recognize, also, that the country wasn't always desert but once had been fertile enough to support populations of horses. Mohammed, the Prophet, believed that Allah had created the Arabian horse from a handful of south wind and called it "drinker of the wind." Certainly anyone comparing this handsome animal with Przewalski's horse or a Tarpan would see only a very basic relationship. It is like comparing a ballet dancer with a professional wrestler.

Although small and lean, the pure Arabian had exceptional strength, speed, and stamina. Its intelligence and patience were far superior to horses of the northern countries, which are often referred to as "cold-blooded." Sensitive, alert, and high-spirited, the Arabian is "hot-blooded." And it has had the unique ability, when crossbred to other types, to pass on its desirable qualities to its descendants, and its bloodline has contributed to producing the most magnificent and famous—as well as the fastest—riding horses in the world. Arabian ancestry sired Alexander the Great's Bucephalus, after which a city was named, Napoleon's Marengo, the Duke of Wellington's Copenhagen, Balaclava ridden by the Earl of Cardigan in the charge of the Light Brigade, Robert E. Lee's Traveller, which is buried on the grounds of Washington and Lee University in Virginia, and every horse that runs in the Kentucky Derby!

It took many centuries for early man to appreciate the full potential of the horse. At first it was just another wild animal to be hunted, killed, and eaten. At the site of a village of Paleolithic hunters near Lyons, France, dated 5000 B.C., the fossils of over a hundred thousand horses have been found. Also discovered was evidence that dogs had been domesticated as early as 7000 B.C., then sheep, goats, and cattle by 4000 B.C. The dog was not man's *first* friend, however; a relative of the horse, the Asiatic onager (donkey or jackass) was domesticated in 10,000 B.C. and was used as a draft animal. The mares provided milk.

Perhaps primitive man's success with the small and slow donkey inspired his attempts to tame the larger and faster horse. Since it was stronger, it could pull heavier loads, and if needed for food, it would furnish more meat. In the beginning, little thought apparently was given to riding on the back of one of these powerful creatures. Persian art from 4000 B.C. shows horses pulling carts, some of which have huts on them, obviously for use as living quarters on long journeys—the first travel trailers! But there was as yet no evidence of men on horseback.

As tribal populations expanded and wars of conquest became more frequent, the horse assumed a new role in history. It gave an army mobility by hauling heavy equipment. Also, the cart with solid wheels was refined and became a light, spoke-wheeled chariot carrying a driver and a warrior, and a two-horse team pulled it into battle at full gallop. It was almost impossible for foot soldiers to withstand the thundering and demoralizing charge of massed chariots bearing down on them at high speed. With this new weapon, in 2000 B.C. an Iranian tribe quickly conquered Syria. Later the Hyksos of Persia overran Palestine and Egypt, using three-man chariots, each carrying a driver flanked by two warriors. The chariot had one disadvantage, however; it was most efficient on smooth terrain and was of little use in mountainous country such as that of southern Greece. The Macedonians (of what is now Greece) developed another means of warfare involving the horse—the cavalry—and it soon superseded the chariot, although eventually the four-horse chariot race became one of the most popular events in the Grecian Olympic games.

It can't be said that the Macedonian armies introduced the use of cavalry in warfare, but they were the first to develop it into an organized military unit. The first men to ride horses probably were those who had to round up the domestic herds from pasture, a task that would be almost impossible on foot. A statue of a horse and rider, found in Egypt, has been carbondated 2000 B.C. A glimpse of a mounted mountain tribesman might have inspired the Greek legend of the centaur, a beast half horse and half man.

The desert tribesmen, using hit-and-run military tactics, preferred riding to chariots because of the speed and maneuverability of their light Arabian horses, and when pursued by an enemy, either on foot or in chariots, they could easily find refuge in the desert where they couldn't be followed. Philip

Superstitious tribesmen who saw the first man riding a horse believed it was a centaur, *half man and half horse.*

of Macedonia, who created the Macedonian army in the fourth century B.C., trained horsemen for use as cavalry, and his successor, Alexander the Great, proved the effectiveness of this new weapon. Mounted on light, fast horses bred from desert stock, his bowmen easily out-maneuvered the more unwieldy chariots of the enemy and conquered the Near East and Egypt and the remainder of the entire civilized world.

The Romans used cavalry simply as an auxiliary of their armies, composed of men from conquered tribes, and in battle preferred the phalanx (massed infantry with interlocked shields). Their tactics did not change when in the second century B.C. they were defeated by Hannibal of Carthage who was aided by an army of thousands of Numidian horsemen. In the fourth century the cavalry of the Goths from the north decimated a large Roman army commanded by Emperor Valens, killing over 40,000 men and the Emperor himself. It was one of the first uses of *heavy* cavalry—men with mail armor mounted on the larger, sturdier horses of the northern woods and armed with heavy spears. Then in the fifth century the Huns from Mongolia, led by Attila, the "scourge of God," swept over Northern Europe as far as France, bringing a new and most important invention—the stirrup.

The mouth bit to control a horse was first used by the first horsemen, and the Gauls in the Roman cavalry designed one that is remarkably similar to a type used today. The first horseman probably rode bareback, as did many of Alexander's cavalry. Then came a saddlecloth, later padded for more comfort. Germanic tribes rode on stuffed cushions. But the Goth heavy cavalry, charging with heavy spears, needed a more secure seat so they wouldn't be unhorsed on impact, and they designed one of the first saddles with a tree (wooden frame) and a high cantle (back).

Early horsemen rode bare and bareback, as shown by this Grecian vase painting of a plump boy trying to mount a large horse.

The early Romans tried the first horseshoe for protecting the horses' hooves on their hard highways; it was the *hipposandal*, an iron boot that was fitted over the hoof and strapped around the ankle. An iron horseshoe, nailed to the hoof, was attempted in western Europe in the first century. It is strange that in over 2,000 years of horsemanship, no one in the western countries thought of a device as obvious and simple as the stirrup! However, once introduced, it was quickly copied by horsemen everywhere.

Another important event in the history of the horse occurred in the eighth century—the introduction of the Arabian to Western Europe. The Moors, riding their Arabians, had conquered North Africa, and in Morocco they had been joined by the Berber tribesmen who rode another important ancestor of the modern horse called the Barb, the origin of which is in doubt although most authorities believe it was a close relative of the Arabian. Then they crossed the Mediterranean and conquered almost all of Spain, which had been occupied by the Goths.

In the open fields their light, agile cavalry easily overcame the Goths who were mounted on large, cumbersome horses, probably a cross between the Tarpan and the huge northern horse. Only in the northern mountains did they fail. The Spaniards realized that the superiority of the invaders was due to their horses, and began to breed similar types. Their own riding horses had been refinements of Tarpan crosses, due to the introduction of eastern stallions by the Romans, and now there was added the blood of the Arabians and Barbs. The result was a strain faster than the Arabian, larger and with more stamina. With it, they eventually drove the Moors back to Africa. It was the horse that became our mustang and Indian pony.

During the eleventh to thirteenth centuries were the Crusades in which Frankish knights with armor of mail rode slow, ponderous horses, descendants of *Equus robustus*, against the Moslems to rescue the Holy Land. They were almost helpless against the fast-riding Moslems mounted on Arabians, who rode around them Indian style, firing arrows to injure the invaders' horses and put them out of action. The Crusaders' eventual victory was due mostly to foot soldiers armed with crossbows which had greater range than conventional arrows and so could keep the Moorish cavalry at a safe distance.

In 1346 the English invented the long bow which could penetrate mail armor. Steel plates were substituted for the chain mail, and even the horses wore armor. And to carry the extra load, *Equus robustus* itself was needed, and the knight became a clanking, miniature castle mounted on a beast that could barely manage a slow gallop without becoming exhausted. The invention of gunpowder and cannon relegated knighthood to the tournament field, and eventually even blunted spears and swords were used to make jousting a safer sport. But the knight's huge, powerful horse is still with us. It has become the Belgian, Shire, Suffolk, Percheron, and the handsome Scottish Clydesdale, a team of which now pulls the Anheuser-Busch brewery wagon.

Originally, the islands of Britain had no horses since they had no land bridge with the continent. Some Tarpan must have reached them through traders, and the Romans added their breeds to the number. When William of Normandy crossed the Channel, conquered England and became its king in 1066, he found its horses too small for his armored men, and imported many large stallions from Europe which later became the mounts of the English knights. But the country's greatest contribution to the horse's development is a fairly recent one, and it was not inspired by war.

The British wanted the best horses for racing, jumping, and hunting, sports in which they had been interested since the days of the Romans. Between 1690 and 1725, three sportsmen imported a trio of the finest—an Arabian (Darley), a Barb (Godolphin), and a Turk (Byerly)—and these were bred to larger local mares. Then their offspring were selectively bred to other Arabian types until finally a new breed was established. No other horse could outrun it or outjump it. It has been called the *Thoroughbred*, which is the breed name; it does not mean purebred. To carry the registry, a horse's ancestry must be traceable to one or more of the three original horses. Now bred in great numbers in the United States, it is the American race horse (except for harness racing).

2. Cowboys and Indians—and Dudes

Until the horse returned to America early in the sixteenth century, the Indian nations had been severely handicapped in their development by the lack of transportation. Their only methods of travel had been on foot or by canoe. They hunted by stalking their prey until it was within reach of their arrows, and these were close distances because their primitive weapons were neither accurate nor lethal at long range. The herds of buffalo, elk, and other animals roamed the country practically unmolested. The tribes generally lived in small isolated villages, subsisting mostly on crops such as maize (Indian corn), which was unknown on other continents and might be considered the Indian's contribution to Europe in exchange for the horse. When a village had to move to another location, the squaws did the hauling, each pulling her family's folded teepee, blankets, and other possessions on a *travois*, a frame made of poles, while the brave walked by her side alert for danger.

Columbus brought the first few horses to the West Indies. On his first voyage all died of exposure and thirst, but on his second crossing the wind and weather were more favorable and he landed his horses at the new colony of Isabella. It was here that the reaction of the Indians, who thought the horses

were savage, man-eating beasts and who ran from them in
panic, convinced him that only with an adequate number of
horses could the New World be conquered. But the supply in
Spain was low, especially of breeding mares. Wars had de-
pleted the stock, and what remained could be sold at high
prices to other European countries which had begun to recognize the value of their Arabian ancestry.

In 1497, with a few hundred stallions and mares, royal
breeding farms were finally established on Hispaniola, the is-
land that is now Haiti and the Dominican Republic. Similar
farms were started on Puerto Rico in 1510, Cuba in 1511, and
Jamaica in 1515. Horses to stock them were supplied by Spain
on condition that equal numbers would be returned from those
bred. Many that left Spain never reached the West Indies. En
route across the Atlantic, the ships followed the shortest course
which took them between the northeast trade winds and the
prevailing westerlies, an area which frequently was dead calm.
With no winds to drive them, the ships remained motionless
sometimes for days, and the horses died by the hundreds. This
stretch of ocean is still referred to as the "horse latitudes."

Enough reached the islands to stock the farms. Cattle ranch-
ing also became a profitable business; the pasture was good
and there were no predators to harm the animals. The beef
sold at high prices back in Spain, and it also fed the Conquis-
tadores on their invasions of the mainland. It is not known how
many of these Arabian-blooded Spanish crosses were raised on
these farms, but many thousand were used for the conquest of
Mexico and Central America and for the settlement of the
Southern United States.

Cortez was the first to be lured by rumors of cities of gold in
the West. In 1519, with 508 soldiers and sixteen horses—the
first horses on the American mainland since 7000 B.C.—he
landed on the shore of Mexico and marched inland, easily
overcoming the opposing Indian armies. The savages fought
valiantly against his swords, crossbows, and muskets, but the
horses demoralized them completely. One horse was killed, but
a supply ship brought Cortez ten more. In his battles, his only
problem was to maneuver his enemy into a position where he
could use his cavalry. On one occasion, according to a historian

in his army, his twenty-five horsemen routed a force of Indians estimated at 50,000!

When he reached the Aztec capital, now Mexico City, Montezuma believed him a god fulfilling a prophecy, and thought his horses and muskets were supernatural. Leaving in peace, Cortez returned to the islands for reinforcements, then attacked Montezuma with 1,200 soldiers and ninety-seven horsemen. His losses were heavy, mostly because the terrain handicapped his cavalry, but he was victorious and returned to Havana laden with quantities of gold and jewels.

His success encouraged other adventurers. In 1521 Ponce de León sailed to Florida but was driven back by the Indians. His inability to use his fifty horsemen in the swamps and brush was the deciding factor. A few years later Vasquez de Ayllon also failed to penetrate to the eastern coast of Florida, his horses also unusable. In 1539 the army of De Soto, with 213 horses, sailed to Tampa on the west coast and fought its way north, then west through Alabama and Mississippi, finally crossing the Mississippi River, but found no gold. After De Soto's death on the shore of the river, his men built boats, released their last five horses, and set sail for the Gulf of Mexico. From their boats, they watched the Indians kill the horses. Neither did Coronado's later expedition find gold when he explored Northern Mexico, and the southern area of the United States.

A popular myth is that horses abandoned by De Soto and Coronado were the basis for the wild herds of mustangs that later filled the plains and were used by the Indians. But De Soto's men had watched their five released horses being killed, and records show that Coronado had only a few mares in his expedition. Ignorant of horse culture, the Indians certainly would not have been able to breed and train them, even if they had obtained a few from the early explorers. The wild herds (called *broncos,* meaning "unbroken") did not appear until two hundred years later.

The Indians actually obtained horses and their knowledge of horsemanship from Spanish settlers and missions. Although in northern Mexico and the southern United States the explorers did not discover treasure like that of the Aztecs, in many

*Monument of an Indian rider in Kansas City, Missouri, a tribute to
the Indians who rivaled the Moors in horsemanship.*

places they did find precious metal waiting to be mined, and
mining towns soon flourished. Since the towns needed food,
cattle ranches grew, and these brought more settlers and missions to convert the heathen Indian. By 1650 there were
dozens of large missions and schools in the New Mexico area
alone, and a similar number of settlements. Indians of friendly
tribes were hired for numerous manual chores, including working in the stables and caring for the horses, and eventually
many were trained as *vaqueros*, or cowboys, to manage the
cattle. Some were given horses, others traded hides, moccasins,
and blankets for them. Still others simply stole them. Frequently, entire herds mysteriously disappeared.

The Pueblos were one of the first southwestern tribes to learn about horses from the Spaniards, and they passed on their knowledge to their neighbors, principally the Apaches. In the late seventeenth century some of the Spanish settlements were raided and thousands of horses were stolen. Gradually, by trade and warfare, the horse spread among the Plains Indians, including the Sioux, Comanches, and Cherokees, then north through the entire western Indian world.

The horse completely changed the Indian's life style. Once confined to a small village and dependent upon an agrarian society, he became a nomad and hunter. His huts were replaced by portable teepees, and a horse, not his squaw, pulled his possessions lashed to a *travois;* he could move his entire village to a distant hunting ground in a single day. His wealth was measured by the number of horses he owned. No wild animal could run fast enough to escape him. He could gallop alongside a fleeing buffalo and shoot it with an arrow at point-blank range; if the animal didn't fall, he plucked out the arrow and shot it again.

The family duffle, tied to a travois, *was pulled by the squaw until she was replaced by the horse.* (Photo Courtesy Museum of the American Indian, Heye Foundation.)

By the eighteenth century, the riding skill of the Indians was equal to that of the ancient Moors who had ridden their Arabians against the Crusaders. And they used a similar technique in their battles with the white man, shooting their arrows while riding at high speed around a settlement, wagon train, or a troop of U. S. Cavalry which had dismounted so its men could shoot their firearms more accurately. The Comanche was probably the best of all Indian horsemen; he used a trick unknown even to the Moors. While attacking, he would slide down the side of his horse so he would be shielded by his horse's body except for one foot, and he would shoot his arrows below the horse's neck. His favorite peace-time sport was horse racing.

The Indian light-horse cavalry became so mobile, and had so many horses, that a new military tactic was developed which had been overlooked by all other cavalry throughout history; one that enabled the tribes to escape the U.S. troopers many times when warned of their approach. Each trooper had only one horse, but each Indian had three or four. When pursued, he would ride one for several hours then change to a fresh mount, while those of the U. S. Cavalry eventually became exhausted. Most victories over the Indians were accomplished by attacking their villages without warning.

The Indians had copied the Spaniard's equipment. Although some rode only on blankets, others had saddles made with wooden frames covered with stretched rawhide. The stirrups were leather-covered wood tied to the saddle with thongs. A loop around the horse's lower jaw usually was the only rein control, used for halting. The Indian, like the Moors in still another respect, directed his mount by leg pressure, leaving his hands free for his bow. The Apaches even devised leather armor, similar to the metal type used by the Spaniards.

During the 1800s almost two million mustangs ranged through the Mid-western prairies. The existence of this wild herd, which had bred for over a century, was due mostly to mismanagement by the Indians. Although excellent horsemen, they had no love of horses. When a colt, born in an Indian herd, couldn't be trained easily or became sickly or lame, it was turned loose to run wild. It was killed and eaten only when food was scarce.

An Indian herd was left to fare for itself in winter; if some became lost, they were seldom missed. When a tribe needed horses, it stole those of another tribe; in the process, many escaped. In a surprise raid, the first objective of the attackers was to stampede its enemy's herd to immobilize its warriors, and these horses fled into the prairies.

Most of an Indian's horses were those he had reared himself, or stolen. Only as a last resort would he attempt to tame a wild mustang. When he did so, he would lasso the mustang and tighten the noose around its neck until it collapsed from suffocation, then he would hobble it and let it stand without food or water for a day or more. This was referred to by the early settlers as "gentling." Afterward, it was ridden back and forth through a swamp or shallow river until the remainder of its spirit was broken. To enable their horses to breathe more easily and so run faster, the Sioux and Comanches frequently split their horses' nostrils to widen them.

Generally, the Indian cared little for his horses as long as they remained healthy and easy to control. He knew nothing of horse culture or breeding for specific qualities. The notable exception was the Nez Percé tribe of the Calouse River region in the Pacific Northwest. The California Mexicans had received some horses of a strange spotted variety which had been bred years previously in eastern Europe, and a few of these were acquired by the Nez Percé. By carefully segregating them and by gelding (castrating) nonconforming stallions so they couldn't breed, they established a distinctive type larger than the mustang, more intelligent and gentle, and so splashed with color that today it is often called the circus or parade horse—the *Appaloosa*. It is considered one of the most beautiful of the modern riding horses.

In the American colonies, the development of the horse followed a completely different pattern. All the horses came from Western Europe. From New England south through Pennsylvania, the demand was for strong draft horses to pull farm plows and wagons, and they continued in use until the 1920s when they were finally replaced by the internal combustion and steam engines. During the expansion westward, they

This Nez Percé Indian has painted stripes over the spots on his Appaloosa. He has no stirrups or saddle. His "pony" is controlled by a rope tied to its nose band. (Photo Courtesy Museum of the American Indian, Heye Foundation.)

hauled the covered wagons (named Conestoga after a town in Pennsylvania), and worked the western farms. Along with mules, which also became popular draft animals, they hauled armament and supply wagons in all America's wars from the French and Indian War until and including World War I. In the eastern cities of the early 1900s they moved the omnibuses, freight wagons, and even the flame-spouting fire trucks. Now the purebred Percherons, Shires, and Clydesdales, sires of these draft horses which helped build America, are bred in small numbers almost exclusively for show. Occasionally, however, a lucky tourist in New England or eastern Canada can still see pairs of these powerful animals in weight-pulling contests.

Not all colonial horses were of the draft type. At first all local transportation was by boat or locally on foot, but gradually the roads stretched inland and riding horses with varying amounts of Arabian blood were imported from England. Some were used for rounding up cattle on northern ranches; the first American cowboys were not Texans but *vaqueros* from Jamaica. One type of horse imported from Canada became

The favorite "cow pony" of the cowboy was the Quarter Horse, *a breed that originated in the South.* (American Quarter Horse Association.)

known as the Narrangansett Pacer; it had a very fast pacing gait. Although horse racing had long been popular in England, it was banned as sinful in puritan New England. One man was ostracized from the church simply for owning a Thoroughbred. But the sight of a doctor, or even a clergyman, dashing through town in his two-wheeled buggy drawn by a fast pacer stirred the gambling blood of the New Englanders, and "drag" races were held secretly. In the early eighteenth century pacing races were finally permitted, the pacer absolved from sin because it could be used for legitimate transportation as well as sport.

Then the trotter was bred from a natural trotting horse named Messenger of Thoroughbred ancestry, and became New York's contribution to racing. Both of these harness racers are now known as *Standardbreds*. The only qualification for a pacer or trotter to carry this name is speed. A pacer must be able to run a mile in 2 minutes 25 seconds; a trotter a mile in 2 minutes 30 seconds.

In the late eighteenth century, a Vermont farmer named Justin Morgan accepted, against his better judgment, in partial payment for a bad debt a young stallion so strange looking that his neighbors enjoyed making fun of its outlandish "figger." Finally Morgan named it Figure. It was pony size with a chunky body too large for its short legs, a deep chest, and weirdly muscular shoulders and hindquarters. A farm hand decided it might be good for something and started to train it. The results were sensational. It became the first of one of America's most famous and valuable breeds—the *Morgan*. Figure had the tremendous strength of a large draft horse, as a trotter it beat all challengers, was intelligent and easy to control and, most important, it had the ability to transmit these attributes to its numerous offspring, which soon were in demand throughout the country.

The Indian tribes east of the Mississippi River never became as interested or dependent upon horses as did their western brothers, primarily because of the dense forests and mountainous terrain as well as their principle occupation of farming. They killed and ate strays that wandered into their crops. The southern Chickasaws were an exception. Even before colonial times they had obtained horses and learned horsemanship from the Spaniards, especially from the Franciscan missions in Georgia. These horses became one of the main sources of supply for the southern colonies.

In Virginia, the Carolinas, and Georgia there were no religious restrictions on horse racing, and the colonists continued to enjoy their Old Country sport of flat racing. But in their sparsely settled farmlands, full-length tracks were impractical because they would be widely scattered and spectators would have to travel long distances to reach them. Therefore they designed numerous short ones, a quarter-mile in length. Since for these they needed sprint horses, they crossed their Chickasaw horses with imported Thoroughbreds, and the result was the *Quarter Horse,* so fast it could beat even Thoroughbreds on their shorter tracks. It later became the cowboy's favorite "cow pony," and the most agile and sure-footed became his cutting horse, used to cut cattle from a herd. Today, with unusual "cow sense," it is one of the spectacular performers at a rodeo. It is also the modern polo pony. To train his racers, the Southerner often used a long whip, the crack of which an unresponsive horse soon learned to recognize. Since it was most common in Georgia, horsemen of that state became known as "Georgia crackers."

Kentucky produced its own all-American breed, the *Saddle Horse,* a mixture of Thoroughbred and Standardbred, unusual for its five gaits. After the Civil War, Tennessee combined the Saddle Horse and Morgan and bred still another type, the *Tennessee Walking Horse* with three gaits, the most unusual of which is a running walk, so smooth that its rider can hold a glass of water in his hand without spilling it.

The first western cowboys were the Texans, and during the twenty years following the Civil War they moved almost 6 million cattle across the plains to the railroad depots in the north. It was a lucrative business; longhorns sold for two dollars a head in Texas and brought as much as forty dollars in Kansas City.

There is little similarity between the cowboy of the 1800s and that of the modern Western movie. When driving a herd, he used from seven to ten horses! He rode one in the morning,

Modern Western horsemen still ride cowboy style, although their choice of mounts may differ. This one is an American Saddlebred. (American Saddle Horse Breeders Association.)

changed to a fresh one at noon, then rested both during the following day. They had a quiet, ambling gait with no quick moves that could startle the cattle into a stampede. He also had a night horse, a swimming horse, a "girling" horse that would walk sedately alongside one ridden by his girl friend, and even a "drinking" horse that would carry him slowly and safely back to his camp after he'd spent an evening in a local tavern.

To impress villagers, he might ride into town on a half-wild bronco. To "break" an untamed mustang he usually hired a professional bronco-buster for five dollars. His prize horse for roundups was the Quarter Horse, when he could afford to buy one for forty dollars or more; the common range horse cost only ten dollars.

Although the cowboys eventually acquired an increasing number of Quarter Horses for their roundups, they were never the beautiful animals shown in the movies; they usually were lean, scrawny, all shapes and sizes. Today's movie "mustangs" are really crossed Morgans and Thoroughbreds, handsome and tall, carefully trained by professional stables and able to rear and "fall dead" at a hand signal or twitch of the reins. The movie hero's cowboy clothing is authentic, although he wasn't always clean-shaven and dressed in white while the mustached outlaw wore black. His ten-gallon hat protected him from the hot sun, could be used as a dipper for drinking water and also as a pillow at night. Leather chaps protected his legs from thorns and cactus and gave him a better grip on the saddle. His neckerchief absorbed perspiration, covered his face to filter out dust, and served as a towel. His lariat not only roped cattle, it tethered his pony and hung horse thieves. The high heels on his boots kept his feet from slipping through the large stirrups, and also dug into the ground to anchor him when he was hanging on to a roped steer. His large silver spurs were mostly for show, but they also enabled his horse to recognize their jingle at night. Long hair was the fashion, not only because barbers were scarce but also for pride; even the Indians considered it a sign of manhood.

The horse population of the United States declined sharply with the advent of the automotive engine. Horses were no longer required in agriculture or transportation. Most of the mustangs that still ranged throughout the West and Southwest were killed for dog food and to supply the fox and mink ranches. Not until the Wild Horses Act of 1971 were the few remaining protected by law. But once again, America is discovering the horse. Its numbers have grown to over six million. In today's mechanized society, our escape is back to nature, and we are learning that there is no easier nor more fulfilling way than to mount a fine horse and ride, however briefly, and to realize that riding with us are the shadows of the great adventurers of history who directed our destiny.

3. The Language of Horsemanship

As a horseman, you must learn "horse talk" by adding a number of new words to your vocabulary. Like all other sports and hobbies, horsemanship has its own terminology. In baseball, you might know what is meant by "the hole behind second base," or a "post pattern" in football. But what is a horse's "frog"? Or a "mouse-dun fillet rising four"? Let's start at the beginning.

To the average pedestrian, a horse is just a horse. But to a horseman, if it's a male less than three years old, it's a *colt;* older than three, it's a *stallion.* Some stallions are neutered so they can't breed. This also makes them more tractable, quieter, and easier to handle, and they usually are safer and less excitable riding horses, less inclined to fight with each other. These are called *geldings.*

A female less than three years old is a *filly;* older than three it is a *mare.* A new-born horse is a *foal.* When a mare has *foaled* (given birth) at least once, it is a *dam,* and if the offspring are so desirable the dam is allowed to foal on successive years, it becomes a *brood mare.*

A one-year-old horse is a *yearling.* An unusual exception is used to designate the age of one of the Thoroughbred breed; its birthday is considered to be the first January 1st after it was foaled. Therefore, it might have been foaled in October, but on the following New Year's Day it is a yearling, although actually less than three months old.

A horse approaching its birthday is said to be *rising;* after its birthday, it is *off.* For example, if it is almost four years old, it is *rising four;* after its fourth birthday, it is *four off.* When it is nine years old, it is *aged,* which means past its prime.

Mares were preferred for warfare by the Moors, and later by the Indians, because they were lighter, more agile, and easier to control by leg pressure, but most of the world's cavalry rode stallions or geldings, preferring to keep their valuable mares for breeding. The Moors were amused by the Crusaders, mounted on their huge stallions which would halt in the middle of a heated battle to *micturate* (urinate), a habit not shared by the mares.

In the Old West, and even sometimes today, a herd of horses left to graze in open land was accompanied by an old mare with a bell around her neck, called a *bell mare.* She was a kind of herd boss. Not only did the tinkle of her bell help riders locate the horses in the darkness, but when she decided grazing time was over, she would head back to camp and the rest of the herd would obediently trot along behind her.

To indicate a horse's height, the term used by horsemen is the *hand,* a unit measuring 4 inches. Therefore, a horse of 16 hands is 64 inches in height (16×4), or 5 feet 4 inches. If the height involves a fraction of a hand—such as 16 hands 3 inches —it is written 16:3, equivalent to 67 inches ($16 \times 4 + 3$). Height is measured from the bottom of the front hoof to the *withers,* which is the top point above the shoulder.

A horseman also refers to the left side of a horse as the *near side,* and the left hind foot as the *near hind foot,* simply because the horse usually is approached and mounted from the left side. The right side is the *off side,* but don't be misled by this term; it doesn't mean riders dismount on this side. A more accurate term probably would be *far side,* but this isn't used.

The various parts of a horse are called its *points;* together they constitute its *conformation.* An experienced horseman can evaluate these points at a glance, and some of them tell him much about the horse's personality and performance.

Points of a horse:

1	Poll	7	Fetlock joint	13	Sheathe	18	Fetlock
2	Forelock	8	Pastern	14	Stifle	19	Dock
3	Arm	9	Coronet	15	Gaskin	20	Croup
4	Forearm	10	Elbow	16	Hock	21	Withers
5	Knee	11	Barrel	17	Cannon	22	Crest
6	Cannon	12	Flank				

(American Quarter Horse Association.)

Most important are the eyes because they reveal the horse's temperament, which is true of most animals and even people. In a riding horse, they should be calm, large, and show intelligence. Ride at your own risk a horse with wild, small, glaring eyes, or eyes with white showing around the pupils; these are signs of temper and meanness.

Understanding a horse's vision helps explain some of the animal's habits which, at times, may be mystifying. Its eyes, among mammals second in size only to the whale's, are extremely complex, with a number of disadvantages as well as advantages. Their pupils aren't round, as are those of most animals, but are elongated, and so the horse can see forward and backward at the same time. In addition, the eyes can rotate separately in semicircles. And they are somewhat like bifocal glasses; the top areas can focus on distant objects and the bottom areas on close objects, also at the same time. Their distant vision is excellent, as is their night vision; in a light at night they shine like those of a deer or cat.

Since the eyes are situated at the sides of the head, however, and both can't see the same object at the same time clearly, especially if it's close, the horse's binocular vision (ability to judge distances) is poor. On rough ground, an intelligent horse will often turn its head sideways, using one eye to watch for and avoid obstacles. When confronted by a hurdle, especially a strange one, a rider sometimes must signal his horse when to jump. Also, any unusual motion at its side, such as a fluttering white paper, may make the horse shy; since it can't judge distance, size, or speed accurately with just one eye, it can't evaluate the sudden motion and is startled by it.

Of all the horse's senses, hearing is the keenest. The ears swivel in all directions and are efficient sound-collecting funnels, enabling the horse to hear many sounds inaudible to its rider. They indicate temperament, also. When you approach a horse, its ears will turn toward you to catch a familiar sound. When you're mounted and on your way, ears perked forward show confidence and contentment. Ears that keep swiveling indicate confusion. Be on guard when a horse flattens its ears against the back of its head; it's ready to bolt, bite, or kick.

The sense of smell is also well developed, and each horse has certain odors it likes and others it doesn't like. Horses with unusual homing instincts follow their noses as well as recognizable landmarks. Large nostrils are desirable; they don't obstruct breathing and will flare wide during a fast canter. A horse doesn't breathe through its mouth or pant like a dog.

The fine hairs rimming the nostrils and upper lip are more sensitive than a cat's whiskers; they help the horse identify objects by touch, especially when feeding. Combining with the sense of smell, they determine whether a substance feels, as well as smells, good enough to eat. They find the choicest grasses and clover, and the lump of sugar in your palm.

The expression, "Don't look a gift horse in the mouth," means that when you receive something for nothing, don't expect too much or you're apt to be disappointed. It might have originated when a cowboy looked into the mouth of a horse given him as a present and discovered it was an old one—by its teeth which are good indicators of a horse's age.

Soon after a foal is born, its soft *milk teeth* appear, and from the age of three these are gradually replaced by its permanent teeth until at five years it has a *full mouth* (complete set) of twelve incisors or *nippers* in front and twenty-four molars or *cheek teeth* in back, for a total of eighteen on both the top and bottom. The biting surface of each nipper is a small hollow or *cup*, and these wear flat as the horse ages. The cups of the two lower center incisors are flat by the time the horse is six. Then the remainder of the lower-teeth cups disappear at the rate of about a pair a year. Next the upper cups wear away, and none remain when the horse is eleven or twelve.

The surfaces of the molars change, too, but not as noticeably. Sometimes, however, they develop sharp edges, and like humans, horses should see their dentists twice a year. These edges must be *floated* (filed off) so they won't gouge the cheek and hamper the horse's appetite. But horses are luckier than humans; their teeth are seldom bothered by cavities. And they never stop growing, always remaining the same length regardless of age or wear. The open spaces along the gums on the sides of the jaw between the nippers and the molars in the rear are the *bars*—convenient as a place for the bit.

Some of the points of a horse have unusual names which are included in the "horse talk" vocabulary. A *dish-faced* horse is one with a face that is slightly concave when viewed from the side; this feature shows a desirable Arabian heritage. A face that is *Roman-nosed* or convex shows the influence of other bloodlines, but doesn't mean the horse will not be a good rider. Often you'll see a horse, usually a stallion, with a brushlike tuft of coarse hair growing forward from between the ears and, in many cases, hanging down over its eyes; this is its *forelock*. The spot where the horse's backbone joins its head, the nape of the neck, is the *poll*. The high, bony ridge on the back above the shoulders is the *withers.* The horse's body between the fore and hind legs is its *barrel,* and the rounded portion of the back above the hips is the *croup.*

A horse's legs are more complicated than they appear. The forelegs are not connected to the animal's skeleton by bone joints, but only by muscles, and they can move only backward and forward. They aren't exceptionally strong. Their main function is to support the horse's forward weight; the powerful hind legs provide the driving power. Each foreleg has an *elbow* as well as a *knee.* The former is a joint visible as a knob high on the rear of the leg. The knee is in the middle of the leg, but it functions more like a human wrist and can bend only backward.

Technically, all bones and joints of the foreleg below the knee are part of the foot, including the long bone attached to it called the *cannon,* so named because it is hollow and tubular like a cannon barrel. The horse is a miraculously designed living machine, but if it has one imperfection, it is this cannon. It is slender, rigid, and subject to severe stress. Often it must support the entire weight of the running horse and rider which can total over a half ton. Add to this the shock of this weight when the hoof strikes the ground. The joint that connects to the cannon just above the hoof is the *fetlock,* corresponding to human knuckles. Its small bones are remnants of the toes of the prehistoric horse. Two additional small bones and their ligaments join the fetlock to the hoof; these constitute the *pastern.*

The hind legs are attached to the skeleton by hip joints enclosed within the horse's muscular hindquarters. The first visible joint, high up on the leg near the body, is the *stifle,* comparable to a human knee. About midway on the leg is the *hock* joint, actually an ankle. In fact, one of its bones is really a heel. The name has been derived from the ancient Anglo-Saxon word *hoch* meaning "high," referring to the high position of the ankle and heel. The part of the leg between the stifle and hock is similar to the calf of a human leg and is called the *gaskin.* Although the hind legs have extremely strong muscles and do all the work of running, jumping, and pulling, in their design which generates this horsepower, Nature has given them the same frailty as the forelegs—the slender, hollow cannon which connects to the gaskin and hoof. When buying a horse, experienced horsemen select one with legs having the shortest cannons. This minimizes the possibility of injury.

The hoof is also not as simple as it may seem. Most of it is a single overgrown toenail that remains from the horse's prehistoric foot. It consists of a *wall* of hornlike fiber extending from the hairline to the ground and enclosing another fibrous section called a *sole*. In the rear of the hoof the wall turns inward to form the *bars* which, with the wall, cover the foot where it touches the ground. The horseshoe nails are placed between the wall and the sole. Between the bars is a soft, triangular pad with a strange name as well as function; it is called a *frog*, and it acts as a rather efficient shock absorber.

The markings and colors of horses are not technically classified as points, but they do add new words to the vocabulary. A large patch of white on a horse's forehead is a *blaze*.

Face marking is a blaze *with a stripe.*

A star *isn't necessarily star-shaped.*

Sometimes it might extend down the face almost to the nose. A very narrow white line from forehead to nose is a *stripe*. A small white patch on the forehead is a *star*—it doesn't have to be star-shaped; any shape will qualify. In ancient times, however, the value of a horse often depended on how nearly the marking resembled a perfect star. Mohammed, the Prophet, is said to have owned such a horse and believed it had divine power.

Sometimes a horse will have a face that is almost entirely splashed with white. The cowboys called this a *calf face;* the Indians more respectfully termed it a *bald face* and even named their horses in its honor, such as Bald Spirit. Leg markings are easily recognized. A *stocking* is white from the hoof up to the knee (foreleg) or hock (hind leg). A *half stocking* is white halfway up the leg, and a *sock* extends from hoof to fetlock.

Colors of horses can be more confusing. *Black,* for example, means *all* black, the skin as well as the hair. If the delicate hairs around the nose are brown, the horse is a *brown,* not a black. And browns can range from light to dark. Sometimes, however, a true black horse might appear dark brown due to its coat having been bleached by strong sunlight. A *bay* is reddish brown. The lightest bay, a reddish yellow, is a *sandy bay;* a deep red-brown is a *mahogany bay;* a bright mahogany is a *blood bay.* An easy way to distinguish a bay from any other brown horse is that it always has a jet-black mane and tail and, frequently, black legs. A *chestnut* has a range of colors similar to a bay, but its mane and tail are always the same color as its body. A light chestnut, from yellow to red-orange with a mane and tail of the same color as the body, is called a *sorrel.*

A *gray,* colored by a mixture of white and black hairs, can vary from iron-gray to almost white. The foal may be almost black but lightens with age. The truly white horse is rare and is an *albino,* completely colorless except for the eyes which are pink. It is an interesting animal but isn't valued highly by horsemen. *Dun* is a dull tan varying from dark (*mouse dun*) to cream-yellow (*buckskin dun*). These horses have black manes and tails and usually a black stripe down their backs. A *roan* is any solid color with a uniform mixture of hairs of other colors. A *strawberry roan* is a mixture of chestnut and white hairs; a *red roan* is blood bay and white; a *blue roan* is black, white, and red, a combination that produces a bluish shade.

Most of the popular breeds of horses have already been mentioned by name in the previous chapter, but a more detailed description of them will help you recognize and understand one when you're offered it as a riding horse. The *Arabian*, the oldest of the breeds, is the most beautiful and most prized by many riders. It is gentle and intelligent with a graceful and swift, smooth gait. And it isn't difficult to identify. Besides the dished face, its neck is arched gracefully; its small head tapers toward its nose and it has eyes that are large, dark, and spaced wide apart; its ears are small and alert; its long, full tail is held high. It is the most desirable of horses; the dream of many horsemen is someday to own one. Currently, there are more Arabians in America than in all other countries combined.

The *Thoroughbred* is one of the world's fastest animals. Although members of the breed may vary somewhat in size and conformation, they can seldom be mistaken for another kind. The Thoroughbred's dished face shows its Arabian ancestry, and its body has the same majestic appearance although it is larger and more powerful, with a deep, broad chest. Its gait is long and low, it has great endurance and seems never to become tired. Its principal fault is that breeders have concentrated on developing its speed and have paid too little attention to its temperament, which is important to all riders except jockeys. The commonest Thoroughbred colors are brown, black, bay, and chestnut. Don't confuse the word Thoroughbred with the term purebred. It is the name of the breed. Any horse with a pure bloodline is a purebred. (Or any animal. You can have a purebred English setter or Siamese cat.)

There is also the *Standardbred*, used for harness racing, which is not a purebred. To carry the name, it simply has to be fast enough. Since it has no definite bloodlines, it isn't as easy to identify away from the track, but it's almost always chunkier than other breeds, with more muscular legs and a longer head and ears. Although its main occupation is racing, because

This Thoroughbred, *with Sky Budin in the saddle, has never been in a race and has become a good pleasure horse and jumper.*

of mixed ancestry it has never lost its ability to accept new owners and learn a new way of life when asked to do so. It's usually neither fussy nor temperamental, and isn't disappointed when it's not allowed an all-out run. Colors are generally brown, bay, or black and occasionally chestnut. White markings are unusual.

Figure, Justin Morgan's little horse-of-all-trades, is responsible for many of today's Standardbred track stars, and its *Morgan* breed is one of the most popular, especially among Eastern trail riders. It's not as tall and stately as the Thoroughbred but is sure-footed with a powerful stride and the constitution of a bull, and its body is heavy-boned and exceptionally strong. Its large chest is proof of its stamina. It is intelligent; one I knew would not only open the paddock gate but also close it after it left so the other horses couldn't follow! A Morgan is usually gentle if handled gently, but if mistreated by an impatient trainer or rider, it soon shows its resentment.

The *Quarter Horse,* quarter-mile racer developed in the

The Quarter Horse *is even faster than a* Thoroughbred *on a short track.* (American Quarter Horse Association.)

South, is a purebred, but today's breed is a mixture of several bloodlines. The racers look almost like Thoroughbreds; others are compact and bulge with muscles like a Morgan. There is no positive way to identify one from its appearance, only from its performance. It has a short head, wide eyes, a neck of moderate length, a huge chest, and powerful legs. To be certain it's a Quarter Horse, ask it to run. It will accelerate faster than a high-powered sports car, reaching top speed in two jumps. Some carry their heads low, the result of painful restraining devices used by trainers who are convinced a horse with its head held high can't start as fast.

The American *Saddle Horse*, a product of Kentucky, is one of the most versatile horses for the rider, and it excels in almost every respect except racing. It is slick and supple, with a long graceful neck. Its style has been so perfected that it has become the prima donna of the show ring. One type performs three gaits; the trot, walk, and canter. These are familiar to all horses, but the Saddler *dances* them with snappy, high-stepping feet. There is also the five-gaited Saddler which, in addi-

This American Saddle Horse *is My My, six times five-gaited world's grand champion.* (American Saddle Horse Breeders Association.)

tion to these three, has a *stepping gait* and a *rack.* The former is an exaggerated high-kneed walk with a hesitation at every step. The rack is a very fast strut.

Most horsemen agree that the *Tennessee Walker* provides the most comfortable ride. The breed was created by crossing a Saddler with a Morgan; the purpose was to produce an exceptional trotter. But strangely, the offspring refused to trot. Instead, they had an unusual flat-footed walk that could be accelerated into a similar run. This feature was refined until today the Tennessee Walker is considered one of the most desirable pleasure horses. It's also one of the most expensive. Its walk and run are difficult to describe. The legs stretch far ahead; the entire body seems synchronized in a forward movement. The result is a smooth, gliding motion. The running walk is a walk in double time, and the canter is a gallop in slow motion. This breed is usually heavier than the Saddler with a more genial temperament. On a trail ride, ask the outfitter if he has a Tennessee Walker you can hire; it will be a delightful ride you'll never forget.

The spotted Appaloosa, *one of the world's most beautiful horses.*

The *Appaloosa,* a horse developed by the Nez Percé Indians of the Northwest, is a registered breed easily recognized. It looks as though its coat were splattered with paint spots of different colors. Originally it was a fine horse with a generous portion of Arabian blood, but through the years it has been bred mainly for its coloring rather than for its performance. The Indians used it for war and hunting. Good ones resemble the Quarter Horse in conformation. When you ride one, you might not win a prize but you'll certainly attract attention.

Another horse bred mainly for color is the *Palomino,* which also varies in conformation and performance. Its skin is completely black, its tail and mane white, eyes dark, and its coat is bright copper or gold. Sometimes it has white markings on the face and legs. A third very colorful horse is the *Pinto,* the "Old Paint" of the Western cowboys, although the breed isn't limited to America; Pintos can be found throughout the world. In its development in recent years, it has been crossbred with almost all other breeds, and the result has been some very capable, as well as beautiful pleasure horses. Its markings of black on white (*Piebald*), or any other color on white (*Skewbald*),

The Pinto, *or* Paint, *is not only handsome; its performance can match that of most other breeds.* (American Paint Horse Association.)

make it stand out from other horses at a circus, parade, a rodeo, or a polo field.

The Pinto in Western stories and songs is often called a "Pinto pony." Is it a pony or a horse? What exactly is the difference? According to Webster's dictionary, a pony is "a small horse." But most of the Indian ponies weren't so small, nor were the Quarter Horses the cowboys called their "cow ponies," nor were all the "Old Paints." On the other hand, the most famous horse breed in the world, the Arabian, is rather small; why isn't it a pony?

Pony enthusiasts insist that the pony is definitely different from a horse. They point to the fact that throughout history the horse has been changed and crossbred to produce breeds for specific purposes: hauling, racing, trotting, dancing, etc. But ponies are essentially still the primitive breeds that existed centuries ago. Among them are such names as the Shetland, Hackney, Welsh, Connemara, and Icelandic. This is certainly true. Nevertheless, the vocabulary, physical points, markings, and colors applied to horses in this chapter also apply to ponies. And for a technical distinction between a horse and a pony, we can accept the standard of the American Horse Shows Association which states that any horse qualifies as a pony if it isn't more than 14 hands (56 inches) tall. Since they are smaller, ponies can be excellent mounts for young riders. And they can do just about everything a large horse can, except on a smaller scale.

SECTION II
Learning to Ride

4. Understanding Your Horse

Horsemen have a proverb: "A green rider and a green horse are a poor color combination." The horse that you, as a green beginner, will ride won't be green and untrained. It will be one that will forgive you your mistakes. And as you learn horsemanship, you'll be more able to appreciate its training. But first it's important for you to understand a few facts about a horse's mental make-up. Discovering them the hard way—by experience—in some cases can be quite uncomfortable.

For example, offer the gentlest old nag a piece of sugar held between your fingertips instead of lying on the flat palm of your hand, and afterward you'd better count your fingers; you might be missing a couple. It isn't that horses are particularly dangerous. Very rarely will one deliberately attempt to harm its rider. The occasional exception usually is when it has been brutally mishandled. It's simply that you must understand horse habits and psychology.

You'll have to revise a few of your former opinions about horses. They're beautiful, wonderful animals, worthy of everyone's respect and admiration, but they're not over-grown versions of your pet pooch that mourns for you when you're away, wags its tail and licks you happily when you return, and might even save your life should your house catch fire. They're incapable of showing the same kind of loyalty, devotion, and affection toward their human companions. Nor, according to biologists, are they nearly as intelligent. At least they rarely show the same kind of intelligence with which we're familiar in "higher" animals, such as the dog.

Many people, mostly those who know little about horses, are convinced that the horse is plenty smart, no matter what the experts say. As proof, in a steeplechase race a horse will never step on a fallen rider because it would injure him. Actually, it has no concern for the man on the ground; instinctively it's afraid of hurting its feet! It wouldn't step on a fallen dog, either. Nor on a white line on a highway, unless it has been taught that white lines are harmless. A horse will negotiate a rocky trail, carefully avoiding obstacles, for the same reason, not because it's worried about spilling its rider.

In Texas, instead of a gate in the fence enclosing a paddock, a common custom is to set a series of long pipes in the ground lengthwise across the opening; the horses are afraid to step on the curved pipes. It doesn't seem to occur to them to step over them. There are always exceptions, of course, like Hank, a horse I used to ride on ranch hunting trips north of San Antonio. The pipes meant nothing to him. He walked on them as though they were flat ground. But it wasn't intelligence that persuaded him the pipes wouldn't hurt his feet. He must have been led over them several times, against his better judgment, and had learned to overcome his fear of them.

A horse may be considered dumb to be afraid of stepping on white lines or a set of pipes, but to be fair to the animal, it's simply obeying its instinct of self-preservation. At times, however, when horses are alone in familiar surroundings and there is no need for caution, they will show intelligence that mystifies the experts. They may be afraid of walking on pipes, but they're Houdinis at escaping from a stall or paddock. Some can open snaps attached to their tether lines; if the snap is too high on the line, they'll bend down till it's on the floor where they can unsnap it with a hoof. They can open bolts on stall doors, the kind that lift and slide back. Also similar wooden latches on paddock gates, and they can even push a wooden drawbar sideways from its supporting post in a fence until one

Is this horse really affectionate, or simply curious? (American Saddle Horse Breeders Association.)

end drops to the ground.

It seems that through the ages the horse has become so used to serving humans and obeying their orders, it uses its own ability to reason only when there's no one around to tell it what to do. This tendency, together with its one-track mind that can concentrate on only one thing at a time, and its excellent memory, actually make it easy to train. In any situation in which its instincts do not warn it of danger, it does as it's told. Its mind is uncluttered by unrelated problems.

In learning, a horse obeys one of the fundamental laws of psychology: pleasure/pain. It happily will do things that give it pleasure and will avoid those that cause pain. (This law applies to humans, too, but we're too intelligent to obey it. We keep smoking cigarettes although we know they can make us fatally ill.) A horse, its sharp eyes recognizing you across the paddock, will come running, not because of a great personal affection for you but because you always have a piece of sugar or other tidbit to feed it. Or because your arrival means it's about to be permitted to leave the paddock for a delightful canter cross-country; the fact that you'll be on its back is merely incidental. It has learned from experience that your presence will give it pleasure. The horse's effort to avoid pain was used by the wranglers of the Old West who "gentled" mustangs. The wild horse learned that fighting the rider had painful consequences that could be avoided by letting him sit on its back. The "crack" of the long training whip used by the old "Georgia crackers" reminded the horse that obeying a command was preferable to feeling the whip itself.

General George Patton once saw a horse throw his sister. He immediately grabbed a whip, but his sister persuaded him not to beat the animal. Instead, Patton ran a noose from the horse's neck through a cleat in the stable floor, pulled its head down to the cleat. Then he knelt, lifted the horse's ear and yelled into it for several minutes, calling it some most unflattering names. This punishment was almost as painful. A moment later his sister rode off on the very subdued horse which had learned that allowing her to do so was preferable to a repetition of the ear treatment. Some trainers, unfortunately, still believe "spare the whip and spoil the horse," but in recent years almost all—including trainers of other, wilder animals—have discovered that gaining the confidence and trust of the animal by emphasizing the pleasure without resorting to pain is of utmost importance and often all that is needed.

To a horse, more so than to any other animal, discretion is the better part of valor. Its strongest instincts are suspicion and fear, and its usual reaction is to run to escape. This has en-

Mr. Rhythm's intelligence is difficult to deny; he has fifty-three different accomplishments. (American Saddle Horse Breeders Association.)

abled the species to survive since little *Eohippus* appeared 58 million years ago. Bravery is of little use to an animal that has neither fangs nor claws with which to fight an enemy. Man, without his intelligence, would have been even more helpless; he can't run as fast as a horse. In fact, almost the only animal he can outrun is a porcupine! A horse instinctively interprets as being potentially dangerous any entirely new experience— any touch or sight or sound it can't recognize as being harmless. War horses aren't brave; they have been taught to believe that the sounds of battle can be safely ignored. The same is true of a policeman's horse in a big city with its roar of traffic, blast of horns, and shoving crowds of strangers. In these cases, however, such numbing of the animal's natural instincts obviously dulls its spirit for a true horseman. In our Civil War, the Confederacy discovered this when it converted many of its fine, highly trained Saddlers and Quarter Horses into cavalry mounts.

The horse on which you eventually will spend many enjoyable hours in the saddle will have its natural instincts of fear blunted just enough by training to make it manageable and safe. New situations are bound to occur, however, that might not arouse its primitive fear completely, but will make it suspicious and insecure. As you will discover, it will be your responsibility as its rider to quiet its fear, to assure it there's no danger. And this is accomplished by having its complete confidence. This is one of the most important rules of horsemanship. The horse will know if you're afraid, nervous, or unsure by an uncanny sixth sense which all horses seem to have.

As a beginner, of course, you won't be completely at ease and certainly, when you begin to ride, you won't have your mount's confidence, but your beginner's horse will have confidence in its handler who has been offering it a succession of strange humans without horse sense, thus far with no painful results. It might not be the most exciting horse you could ride, but its many experiences will have taught it to be one of the least excitable. When you're an accomplished rider and something happens that tends to panic your more spirited

Consider the intelligent eye of this Arabian.

mount, your attitude and reassurance will avoid a crisis. It might be a calm word, a shift of position in the saddle, a relaxation of your knees, a change of tension on the reins. The horse will sense that you know what you're doing and will trust you.

Don't underestimate a horse's sixth sense. If you're on a ride and your mount suddenly halts, it may have a good reason for doing so. If you do convince it to continue, and it does so nervously, watch out for trouble. Its caution and fear may be unreasonable to you, but they're real and reasonable to the horse. John James Audubon, the famous bird artist, wrote that one day while he was riding through the Kentucky forest, his horse Barro halted and behaved nervously. A few minutes later there was an earthquake, one of the most violent ever experienced in North America, estimated as having been greater than that which years later demolished Anchorage, Alaska. It has since been revealed that horses do actually know when an earthquake is about to occur.

In another true tale, a horse refused to carry its rider along a forest trail at night, and he was forced to return to the nearest village. In the morning he found that a narrow bridge farther along his intended route had been washed away by a flash flood. Many horsemen in areas where winters are severe are certain that horses can sense when the ice on a frozen lake isn't thick enough to carry their weight and will refuse to cross.

If you still don't believe a horse has a sixth sense—a kind of extrasensory perception—ask the man who rides a cow pony. Watch a rodeo and you'll see that many times the horse seems to know what a calf will do before the calf itself knows. Eventually you'll find, too, if you are accustomed to ride the same horse, that it will be reading your mind. At least it will seem so. You will only think about turning, or cantering, and the horse will immediately do so. What actually happens is that the horse has become sensitive to your slightest movements and has learned to interpret them.

When you're about to turn, without being aware of it you might increase slightly the tension on a rein or move it so it touches the horse's neck, or shift your body so you'll be ready to maintain your balance. To prepare to canter, you might rise slightly in the saddle. Ginger, whom I rode on Wyoming trails

This Thoroughbred *"laughs" with pleasure whenever anyone pours water on its head.*

for many years, was a horse with unbelievable sensitivity. Of course, she had learned to know me very well. All I had to do was nod my head "yes" a couple of times and she'd move out. If I nodded to one side, she'd turn in that direction. Sometimes, while riding with companions, I found her extrasensory perception somewhat of a problem. While talking I'd turn toward them, or gesture with my hand, and often Ginger would misinterpret and start to change her gait or turn. I had to learn to give her a quick countersign. The fact that she'd made a mistake never seemed to annoy her.

Since a trained, spirited horse is so sensitive to the slightest disposition of a rider, you can imagine how it must become confused and nervous when ridden by an inexperienced horseman who jumps around in the saddle, tugs on the reins, and kicks his legs. He won't stay on such a horse very long. Pity the poor riding stable nag that must put up with numerous customers every week, sometimes three different ones a day, many of whom have no idea of horsemanship and think all they have to do to be successful horsemen is to kick the horse with their heels to make it move, haul back on the reins as hard as possible to make it stop, and squeeze their legs around it to keep from falling off.

Should you go to a stable to rent a horse for a ride around the park, the handler will ask you if you've had any experience. If you haven't, you'll get one of these poor creatures that have suffered so long all their resistance and spirit have been broken. If you've had experience, you'll get a more sensitive mount, its capabilities depending upon how much horse you can handle. The only way to really learn horsemanship will be for you to take lessons from a competent instructor. He won't start you on a poor numb critter that knows only how to lumber along and stop when shouted at, showing the only signs of spirit when it's headed back toward the stable. Like a fine car you're learning to drive, your beginner's horse will be sensitive to how you handle the controls and so help you to learn them correctly. It will be quiet, well-behaved, alert, and have a willing disposition. It may take a while for you two to know each other, but the friendship will be a happy one.

Important to remember is that a fine horse can sense your attitude while you're still on the ground as well as on its back, so when you approach it, act as though you'd known horses all your life. Appear confident; this will dispel most of the nervousness it may feel about meeting a stranger. The horse will know if you're hesitant or afraid. It's a mistake to approach cautiously as though you were sneaking up on a tethered lion. And don't extend your hand, then when the horse turns its head toward you, yank back your hand as though you expected to be bitten. And don't ask the handler, "Does he bite?" If I were the horse and could understand the question, I think I'd feel I had a right to bite you!

Never make a sudden or abrupt movement near a strange horse; remember it doesn't have stereo vision and might have difficulty understanding your action. Approach it from the front or side where it can always see you. Watch its heels if you have to walk in back of it; since it can't see you it might kick instinctively. Pat it first *gently* on the neck, not on its very sensitive nose until it extends it toward you; a horse is used to being touched on the neck but touching the nose is a more intimate greeting. Talk to it calmly, using its name. Run your hand over its withers. After a few minutes your introduction will be complete and you'll be ready to climb aboard.

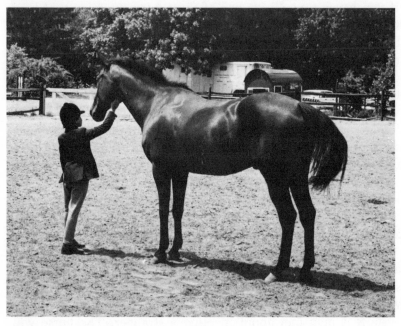

Approach a strange horse with confidence, stroke its neck first, then its nose when it extends it toward you.

5. Your Riding Outfit

If you intend to be a serious horseman or horsewoman, you should wear the proper clothing; it's more important than you may think. Around the stable, or for an occasional short saunter through the pasture, a pair of old dungarees and a sport shirt are excusable; their advantage is that when they become soiled, they're easy to clean. But there are other considerations. Improper clothing cannot only be unattractive, but can be uncomfortable and can hamper your handling of the horse.

If you must wear dungarees or jeans, be sure they fit as tightly as possible around your knees and legs and reach down to your ankles. If they're loose, they will wrinkle and make your knees sore on a long ride because you use your knees to signal your horse. If they're too short, the exposed skin will chafe from rubbing. Cotton or wool gabardine *jodhpurs* are best; they're loose at the hips and seat, then taper to a snug fit over the knees and legs to the ankles. A strap under the sole holds them in position. Stretch breeches, like the old-fashioned knickers, can be worn instead; they're similar to jodhpurs but don't quite reach the ankles. They should fasten tightly around the calf of your leg so they won't slide up and wrinkle. Sneakers are not advisable for footwear. Laced shoes will do, but they should have heels so your feet can't accidentally slide completely through the stirrups. Low jodhpur boots will at least make you look more like a horseman. Most serviceable, handsome, and offering the greatest protection to your legs are riding boots; these should also fit snugly and reach up to a point just below the hollow behind your knees. Loose-fitting Western boots are prettier than they are practical. Clean all leather boots after every ride, using a damp sponge and mild soap. Then apply a leather preservative and finally polish.

For safety, always wear a hard hat, the kind made especially for riders. It has a cushioned lining and an inner head band that is adjustable for size; usually covered with velvet, it is quite attractive and stylish in spite of its serious function. Don't wear a loud shirt; it will brand you as being a duffer. And a string tie is more manageable than the ordinary kind. Your *hacking* jacket for pleasure riding—a light one in summer and a heavier one in winter—should be form-fitting so its bulk won't get in your way. For all riding, wear gloves—porous ones when it's warm and leather when it's cold; they'll keep the reins from slipping through your hand. Spurs? They may give you a more traditional appearance, especially if you're an admirer of Western horsemanship, but they aren't necessary un-

This well-dressed rider, Miss Pat Cuccia, wears a helmet, stretch breeches (jodhpurs), boots, and a light vest when the weather is too hot for a jacket.

less, some future day, you chance to climb on the back of a cantankerous, stubborn critter with the disposition of a mule. Nor will you have to carry a whip, although it might make you look more professional. Don't think a rider with a whip is unnecessarily cruel; it's not for beating the horse. Maybe the horse has been trained to respond to a touch of the whip instead of a heel on its flank. Maybe at a fast gait the rider prefers to use it instead of a heel, which would require moving his or her leg from its balanced position. A riding *crop* looks smart and serves the same purpose. If it has a long brush on its end, it's called a *whisk*, and it also can be used to discourage biting flies which make a horse's life miserable.

It's not economical to buy expensive riding apparel if you're not an adult; you'll outgrow it. But if you are full-grown, buy the best you can afford. Not only will it look better and last longer, but it will also be more comfortable. Naturally, apparel for young people costs less than that for adults.

Your horse's riding outfit is called its *tack* and consists of the equipment it needs in order for you to guide it and ride it comfortably. For your initial lessons, your horse probably will be all *tacked up*—wearing its tack and ready to go when you arrive. To identify these various items of its outfit, you must add a few more words to your horse-talk vocabulary.

The *bridle* is the head harness; its main purpose is to hold the bit in the correct position in the horse's mouth: over the tongue and on the bars between the front incisors and the rear molars. It is held in place by a number of straps. The one over the head behind the ears is the *crown;* attached to it and lying across the forehead is the *brow band.* Extending downward from where these join, and passing under the throat, is the *throat latch.* From the crown, continuing down each cheek and fastening to rings at the end of the bit, are the *cheek straps.* And around the nose, helping to hold them in place, is the *nose band.*

There are several kinds of bits. As a beginner, of course, you will have little rapport with your first horse; it won't be able to read your mind or recognize your habits. But to make your introduction to riding as uncomplicated as possible, the horse probably will be one with a somewhat sensitive mouth, requir-

The horse's bridle that holds the bit in place.

ing the simplest, mildest kind of bit and only one pair of reins. This is the *snaffle*. It is a bar, usually metal, jointed in the middle with a ring at each end to which a rein is fastened.

Some day you may meet a hard-headed horse with a tough mouth and a mind of its own, which won't think too highly of your horsemanship. To persuade it that you're the boss without a lot of weary tugging and yanking on a simple snaffle, you'll use a more severe bit called the *curb* or *Pelham*. It is a snaffle with an unjointed bar and with extensions which give it a shape similar to the letter H. And besides rings at the end of the bar, it has them at the ends of the H, also, making a total of six, three on each side. This H lies almost flat in the horse's mouth, held in this position by a short chain that is attached to the rear rings and passes under the horse's chin. A second pair of reins, called the *curb* reins, is fastened to the front rings; when these are pulled they exert greater pressure in the mouth because they provide more leverage, and the chain is forced

The jointed snaffle, one of the simplest bits.

The Pelham bit with a curb chain is more severe.

upward against the chin. This arrangement isn't as cruel as it
may seem. It's better to pull on a curb bit once and be obeyed,
than to yank a snaffle repeatedly until the horse's mouth becomes sore. You may think that two sets of reins will be
difficult to handle, but you'll be surprised how quickly you'll
become used to them.

If you're an Easterner, the saddle on your first horse will be
the *flat,* or *English* type, and it probably is the kind you'll use
for most of your future experiences as a horseman. Most practical for pleasure riding, it is light, flexible, least tiring to horse
and rider, and will enable you to handle your horse with the
most precision. And because the front *pommel* is low, the rear
cantle curving upward behind the seat, it makes it easier for
you to shift your weight forward when necessary to achieve
the best balance in relation to the horse's center of gravity.

*The flat, or English, saddle with
cinch on the left in the photo.
This model has a high cantle
and low pommel to facilitate the
forward seat.*

Eventually, the *stock* or *Western* saddle may attract you. It
has a romantic history and is all-American, usually attractively
engraved, the type you see in TV Westerns and in rodeos. But
it's expensive, heavy (forty pounds or more), limits your forward movement in the seat and is not considered the first
choice for precision riding. It has a high pommel topped by a
horn which a cowboy or cowgirl can hang onto during a mad

The stock or Western saddle with its deep seat and horn. (Tex Tan.)

ride through the sagebrush, or to which a lariat can be tied to hold a steer. This high pommel, plus the saddle's deep seat, keeps the rider well anchored in one position, however, which often is well behind the horse's center of gravity. The horn discourages you from leaning forward because it threatens to ram you in the belly.

If you're going to rope cattle, you might want a stock saddle. During trail rides up and down mountains it might make you feel more secure; most of the outfitters supply them. And dude ranches. How unromantic it would be for a city slicker, all tacked up like a cowboy with a ten-gallon hat, chaps and spurs, to go riding off into the sunset on an English saddle!

The saddle is constructed basically of a wooden frame called a *tree,* covered with several layers of leather. It's held on the horse by a *girth* or *cinch,* sometimes two, passing under the horse and buckled to the saddle by straps called *billets.* A small leather flap behind the buckles keeps them from scratching the horse, and a leather *saddle skirt* over them shields them from the rider's legs. The stirrup straps, hanging down over the skirt, are held to the saddle by two safety *stirrup bars,* one on each side. These are slotted metal devices with the slots open toward the rear; a loop at the top of the stirrup strap fits into the slot. So you won't worry about falling off your horse and being dragged for miles as you've seen in the movies, a backward pull slides the stirrup strap from the slot and the stirrup drops free. These bars are also covered by a protective leather flap.

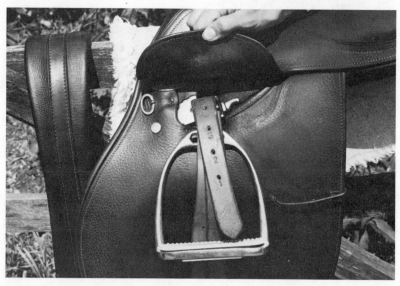

Flap raised to show the stirrup bar, open at the rear so the stirrup leather can pull free should the rider fall.

A harness may have a few additional straps. A common one is the *breastplate,* running across the chest and attached to the cinch; it keeps the saddle from sliding backward on a very slender horse, or on one used for climbing steep mountain trails. The *standing martingale* passes between the horse's forelegs, connecting the cinch and the nose band, and keeps an excited horse from tossing its head which might waste time for a polo player or rodeo rider. A variation for the same purpose is the *running martingale,* similar but instead of fastening to the nose band it splits into a Y at the chest, each end having a ring through which one of the reins passes. Many riders prefer this type to the standing martingale because it is more versatile—its degree of restriction depending on the tension of the reins.

6. Riders Up

Your horse is tacked up and waiting, and it's time for you to mount. Expect to be awkward at first; mounting easily and correctly requires some practice. But your beginner's horse will be patient, more so than many horses you'll ride in the future. It might even let you accidentally kick it in the flank with your right foot once or twice. Mounting involves more than just scrambling into the saddle. Do it the right way, and you'll soon gain the horse's confidence which is so important. While mounting you must steady the horse and keep it from moving, not difficult when you know how. Your instructor or his handler will steady it for you the first few times, but eventually you'll be on your own.

A rider mounts from the near (left) side of the horse. Although there's no logical reason why you can't mount from the right side, doing so will lose you points at a show. You must mount from the near side because it's the way cavalrymen have been doing it through history; their swords, hanging from their left hips, made it difficult for them to mount from the right. Today we no longer wear swords but the custom continues. Standing at your horse's near shoulder, take both reins in your left hand and with the same hand reach up and grasp the saddle's pommel. Or, if it makes you feel more secure, grab the

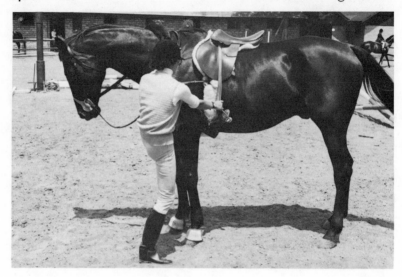

Mounting from the near side. The stirrup is turned so the left foot can be inserted.

mane near the pommel, a generous portion of it; too little will concentrate your pull on a few hairs and they might pull out. Adjust the tension on the reins you're holding. Too tight and the horse might back up; too loose and you might not be able to tighten them quickly should the horse start to move forward. The tension is right when you can just feel the horse's mouth.

Then face the croup (rear). With your right hand turn the left stirrup so the correct side is toward you, and insert your left foot until the ball of the foot rests on its tread, or *iron*, your toes pointing toward the rear. Don't relax your left hand holding the reins and mane. If the stirrup is too high, lengthen it; you can shorten it again after you're in the saddle. Or you can stand on a mounting block or the bar of a fence, or get a boost, called a *leg up*, from a friend. But be careful whom you choose to do the boosting; some jokers think it very funny to boost an unsuspecting novice completely over the horse!

With your foot in the stirrup, grasp the cantle of the saddle with your right hand, push quickly on your right leg and lift your body with your arms and left leg. Push your left knee

With hands on the pommel and cantle, right leg is raised high as it swings over the horse's back.

against the saddle and extend your left foot as you lift and turn, so its toes don't jab the horse's barrel. Release the cantle and swing your right leg high over the horse's back, too low and you might kick it in the flank and have a surprise take-off. Then release the pommel or mane but be careful not to change the tension on the reins; the horse might think you're signaling it to move. Lower yourself gently into the saddle, not with a thump. After you're settled, your instructor will adjust the length of the stirrups; with your legs hanging straight down, the iron should touch the bone of your ankle. Watch him; some day you'll have to do it yourself.

Most important is your *seat*, the way you sit in the saddle. Actually it's more a kind of standing than it is sitting. You rest your weight more on your thighs and legs than on your buttocks. Your back should be straight or slightly convex, body bent forward slightly so your shoulders are directly above or slightly behind your hips. Try to avoid looking down at your horse; you'll lean too far forward. Your left arm, its hand holding the reins (or both arms if you hold one rein in each hand), should be inclined forward slightly, your elbow (or elbows)

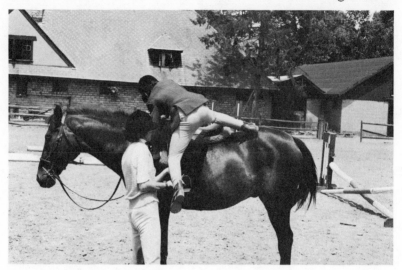

A young rider, too small to mount by himself, gets a "leg up."

bent so it, your hand, and the bit, will be approximately on a straight line. The balls of your feet should press on the stirrup irons with your toes pointing almost straight forward. Your knees will be bent forward slightly and will be directly over the stirrups.

Don't try to wrap your legs around the horse; let them hang down comfortably. But the insides of your legs, just below the knees, should touch the horse's barrel at its widest part because at these points you will be able to apply most successfully the leg pressure (frequently referred to as knee pressure) that will help you signal your horse. The above description of your seat refers to the flat saddle; in a stock saddle the seat is somewhat different but easily learned once you have mastered the basics of riding. One of the differences is *not* that on a stock saddle you must wrap your legs around the horse as you've seen many rodeo riders do, especially the bowlegged ones.

At first you'll probably be instructed to hold one snaffle rein in each hand, the so-called English style. Grasp the rein by holding your open hand above it, thumb toward you, then closing your fingers around the rein and turning your hand so

Most common method of holding a rein in a "fist."

that the thumb is on top. Your hand will form a kind of fist, the rein entering it at its heel near the little finger and coming out at the top where it can lie across your forefinger and be held tightly by the pressure of your thumb. A variation is to place the rein between your little finger and ring finger before closing your hand on it. To hold both reins in one hand, usually the left hand (Western style, so you can hold onto the horn or swing a lariat with your free hand), combine the two methods so that one rein enters your fist between the little finger and ring finger, the second one under the heel of your hand, and both held against your forefinger by your thumb. The loose part of the reins should lie across the horse's back.

The one-hand hold should be used when shortening or lengthening one or both reins either to even their length or adjust their pull against the bit; the adjustments are made with your free hand from *behind* the hand holding the reins which is called the *bridle hand.* To lengthen a rein, your natural impulse will be to reach in front and pull it through the bridle hand, but this is apt to cause a sudden slack which can confuse a sensitive horse. Most horsemen never touch the reins between the bridle hand and the bit. It's best to hold the reins with your free hand behind the bridle hand to steady them, open your bridle hand slightly, then draw this hand back to a new position where the rein or reins are the desired length. To shorten one or both reins, your free hand simply pulls them back through the bridle hand. The rein length is correct when you can just feel the horse's mouth as you tighten the reins very slightly. They may still be too long, however, when you meet a horse that will let you pull them back too far by pulling in its chin. In holding a Pelham bridle, use the one-hand method just described with two reins in each hand, the curb rein on the bottom and the snaffle rein on top. In this case, changing rein length is slightly more difficult, but adjustments are still made from behind with the opposite hand.

Now you're ready to walk. In controlling your horse, you use what in horse-talk are called *aids;* these are the reins, your hands, your legs, and your weight which you shift in the saddle. You use either one of these or a combination of them. Different horses need varying degrees of encouragement to start moving; some hard-headed critters may even have to be nudged by your heels. But your training horse won't require any desperate measures. While you've been getting all squared away in the saddle, it probably has been relaxing, not showing

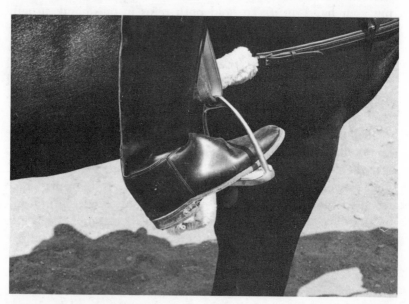

Ball of the foot on the stirrup iron, and a low heel so the ankle can act as a shock absorber when it supports the rider's weight, especially in fast gaits and jumps.

too much interest in what you've been doing. Tighten the reins slightly; this informs it that you're ready to go. This will also bring its head and the bit into the correct position, and your horse will shift its feet to a balanced stance. This is called *collecting* your horse. Now move your weight slightly forward, squeeze its barrel with your knees (actually the calves of your legs below the knees), move the reins forward as it stretches its head forward for the first step.

As your horse walks, its head moves, and so also must your hands to maintain their slight tension on the reins. To accomplish this smoothly, your arms and body must remain relaxed. If you're stiff, the horse will know it and won't like it. Don't try to hang on to the reins to keep your balance. Exert a slight pressure with the balls of your feet against the stirrups. Your legs may flex slightly as the horse moves, but your body above the waist should be erect with only a slight motion of the shoulders.

To turn your horse to the right, lean your weight to the right

Correct body position for walking, the hands moving with the horse's head as it nods.

and move your right hand holding the right rein slightly to the rear, increasing the tension on that rein. This is called a *direct* rein. The left rein should remain as loose as it was during the straight walk. It's not necessary to yank the horse's head around. Often just the increased pull on one side of the bit is sufficient, and the horse will turn its body with only a slight turn of its head. If it needs additional prompting, squeeze its barrel with your right knee to swing its hindquarters to the left. You might also move your right hand out to the right to get a more direct sideways pull; this is called an *open* or *leading rein*. To be still more persuasive, also place your left hand on the horse's withers so the left rein presses against the neck; this is a *bearing rein*.

The bearing rein can also be used to start a walk when you hold both reins in your left hand; press with your knees and immediately bring your left hand to the withers as above. There is no pull on one side of the bit for a turn, only the rein pressure against the left side of the neck which you can vary according to the amount necessary to make your horse move. Responding to the pressure, the horse will take a step sideways to the right. Immediately relax your knees and the left rein, and after that first step your horse will keep walking straight ahead. For a right turn with both reins in your left hand, bring the hand to the horse's withers, thumb uppermost, and flex your hand at the wrist so there's a slight pull on the right rein, and the left rein lies against the horse's neck. If necessary, add some pressure with your right knee as described. All left turns, of course, are made similarly to the right turns by using the opposite reins and pressures.

To stop your horse, lean your weight backward slightly and hold back the reins to keep the horse from nodding its head forward as it must while walking. Sometimes a gentle pull may be necessary. After it has stopped, use knee pressure to collect the horse, then relax the reins. To back up, shorten the reins and hold them tight to maintain a slight but steady pressure on the bit, lean your body to the rear, and squeeze your knees. The knee pressure signals the horse to move, but it can't move forward because of the tight reins. And your shifted weight has moved the balance backward. To restore the balance and move out from under your pressing knees, the horse will step back.

Some riding instructors will require you to mount and dismount several times, to be sure you can perform them without difficulty before teaching you how to walk your horse. Dismounting is also done from the near side. Hold the reins in your left hand and place that hand on the saddle's pommel or grasp a handful of mane as you did when mounting. Be sure the reins aren't too tight; if they are, they will pull on the bit and the horse may decide to back up while you're dismounting. Too loose, and it may move forward. Then remove your right foot from its stirrup and, rising in the saddle, swing the leg over the horse's back and place your right hand flat on the saddle or grasp the cantle. Your legs should hang side-by-side, knees straight. Rest your weight on your hands while you free your left foot from the stirrup. If this seems to require too much muscle, you can rest your weight across the saddle. Finally, slide to the ground, landing gently on both feet. Don't lower your right foot first, leaving your left foot in its stirrup; such gymnastics might cause the horse to move before your

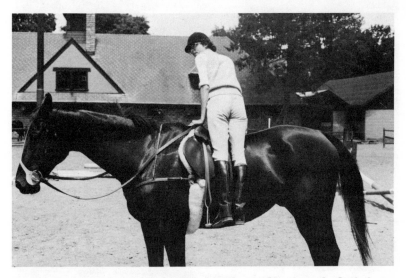

In dismounting, lower your body gently to the ground; don't leave your left foot in the stirrup.

left foot is free and you'll be in trouble.

To lead your horse back to its stable or the handler, stand on the horse's near side and hold the reins with your right hand about six inches below the bit. Loop the remainder of the reins over the horse's withers or hold it in your left hand. Don't let it drag on the ground; you or the horse might trip over it. Walk forward and the horse will walk beside you. If it refuses, with the reins pull its head firmly sideways toward you, then away from you; it will take a step to maintain its balance and once moving will walk. Watch its feet! It might accidentally step on one of yours. Never intentionally, of course.

To make a horse back up when you're leading it, face the rear and stand to the left of its head, your left hand holding the reins short as described above, and pull them toward its chest so it tucks in its chin. At the same time push against its shoulder with your right hand. It will move back reluctantly; it would much rather go forward.

To start your horse moving, you can cluck while you're using the recommended aids, although it won't help unless the horse

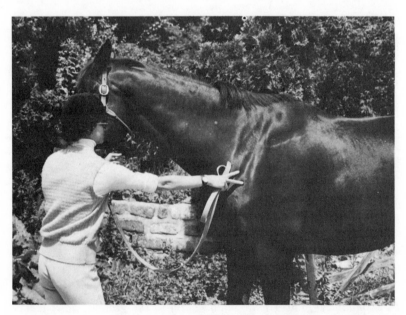

Encouraging a horse to step backward by pressing its shoulder.

is familiar with clucking sounds and knows their purpose. It's not endorsed by sophisticated horsemen; it's considered uncouth. And there's no need to shout "Giddap" at the top of your lungs, unless maybe you're riding a truck horse. A well-trained sensitive horse probably will misunderstand, and such a terrifying shout might treat you to a take-off that's more violent than you expect. And yelling "Whoa" to stop might spur it on to even greater effort. But a horse can learn to recognize these commands, of course, when they're given repeatedly in a calm voice. Old Betsy whom I rode as a boy and who knew me very well had quite a vocabulary. I'd just say "Go" and she'd step out; "Hold it" and she'd stop; "Slow down" and she'd stop trotting or cantering. A number of times I tested her to make sure I wasn't involuntarily using other aids, such as shifting my body or moving my knees. But I could sit perfectly quietly in the saddle, say "Go" and she'd go. Talking to a horse in a soothing tone actually might be considered one of a horseman's aids, not only to quiet it when it becomes excited, but also to show your pleasure when it performs well. It might not know what you're saying, but at least it will realize eventually that you're not such a bad guy, or gal, to be carrying around.

7. The Fast Gaits

After your first few lessons on walking your horse, you'll probably feel you've acquired enough experience to try a trot,
canter, or gallop, but it will be a mistake to be too impatient.
You must be able to walk with precision before you can run
with precision. You must perfect your use of the aids until they
become almost instinctive, requiring very little concentration.
The faster you go, the more important these aids become. And
since, like people, no two horses are the same, while walking
you'll have the opportunity to learn the temperament of your
particular horse and any idiosyncrasies it may have; you'll become used to its rhythm and stride, also discover how firmly
you must use your aids. At the same time, of course, your horse
will be learning all about you and will be acquiring confidence
in you. Eventually you and your horse will be a unit, not two
separate individuals. Some instructors consider the walk so important that they make their students devote a dozen lessons or
more practicing it.

While walking, you can also perfect your seat and your balance. Occasionally ride with your feet out of the stirrups until
you can do it confidently without tugging on the reins for support; this will teach you to sway your body gently forward and
back, bending at the waist, in time with the horse's stride,

which you'll find you must do in order to maintain your balance when your feet hang free. With the horse motionless, stand in the stirrups, balancing yourself with just your legs, not the reins. Then try it walking; at first you'll be able to keep the position for only a couple of steps before you flop back into the saddle. With your instructor's permission, try riding the walk bareback; when you can do it without feeling that you might take a spill at any moment, you'll be well on the way to learning all about balance. Remember that many of the Moors and Indians rode their mounts bareback at a full gallop.

Practice turns by walking in progressively smaller circles, both left and right. Turn in figure-eight patterns of varying sizes. But don't repeat any single monotonous practice maneuver too long at one session; even a horse can become bored and decide there are better things to do. You've been walking your horse slowly; try it slightly faster. Start at a slow walk, then apply a brief squeeze of your knees. Not too much, and don't loosen the reins too much; your horse might break into a fast trot. If it should, tighten the reins to halt it, then try again. It will soon learn your intention. Learn to control your speed by walking alongside a more experienced rider. Stay close, stirrups almost touching and the noses of both horses almost even as in a photo finish at a horse race; don't lag behind or push out ahead for more than a few inches. You'll never need such precision unless you ride in formation at a show, but it's good training.

Try walking up and down hills, too, but not steep ones while you're still an amateur. While climbing, you'll discover just how much slack rein your horse will need, and while descending, how much to tighten it to keep your horse from running. Follow trails that provide good footing. A horse that's used for Western trail riding, of course, will know all about mountains as well as hills and usually the best thing to do is let it have its way. No matter how accomplished a horseman or horsewoman you may become, with each new horse you ride you should spend some time at the walk and other basics to learn its rhythm and response to your aids before taking it on a faster ride. And every horse, just taken from its stable, should be walked at least a mile before being required to trot, canter, or gallop, just as every athlete is allowed a loosening-up period before the big game or race.

The trot is a two-beat gait, the horse's hooves striking the ground in diagonally opposite pairs, for example: the right front hoof and the left hind hoof, and the left front hoof and right hind hoof. Most riders *post* the trot, a method first used in 1870 by an English postman who delivered the mail on horseback; they rise from the saddle while one of these pairs is on the ground, and sit until the same pair touches the ground again. Posting is certainly the most comfortable way to ride the trot, as you will discover, but try it first in a sitting position, the full seat. Done correctly, you will find it need not be as violent an experience as you have imagined, and it will make you aware of your horse's trotting rhythm. Most of the old Western riders sat while trotting, including the Indians for whom posting would be difficult without stirrups. Try to remember how often you've seen a cowboy posting in a Western movie! Modern Westerners still sit; it's easier in a Western saddle.

Put your horse into a fast walk, and when everything is

With your horse stationary, practice posting by rising slightly in the saddle.

under control, use your aids to encourage it to go even faster. Usually, all you have to do is slacken the reins slightly by moving your bridle hand forward; sometimes you must add a momentary nudge with your knees. When the horse responds, immediately shift your weight to the rear of the saddle and lean backward, your body relaxed, legs and feet in the normal position. Resist the temptation to swing them back and clamp them against the horse's flank. Then increase tension on the reins; too much and the horse will slow down to a walk or will stop, too little and it will go into a fast trot. Use just enough tension to maintain a slow trot, at least until you know what to expect. If you're not sitting correctly, you'll soon know it. Lean forward, stiffen your body, push back your legs and you'll bounce up and down like a Yo-yo, eventually giving the reins a yank that will bring your horse to a sliding stop. Then start all over again. To be fair to the cowboys, it must be admitted that sitting the trot is somewhat easier in a traditional Western saddle because of its design which always carries the rider's weight farther to the rear than does a flat saddle.

You'll still be shaken up a little, of course, no matter how you sit, and after you learn to post, your saddle will seem like a padded cushion by comparison. It will also seem that way to the horse. First practice the posting movements when your horse is stationary; if the horse seems to become annoyed by your antics, have a companion steady its head. Sit forward in the saddle so your weight is directly over the stirrups, then rise and sit, rise and sit, in time to your horse's rhythm which you discovered when sitting the trot. It should be a smooth continuous motion, like rocking back and forth in a rocking chair. You rise by supporting your weight on the stirrups and straightening your knees. Don't bend your hips. As you lift your body, it will rock forward. This might seem to upset your balance, but it won't when your horse is actually moving. Return to your seat gently; don't fall down on the saddle.

When you think you understand this rocking motion, try posting while trotting—preferably a slow trot at first. Your movements must synchronize with your horse's two-beat rhythm. If they don't, you'll bounce all over its back. You'll find it easier to rise from the saddle than when the horse was sta-

Posting while trotting. Here the rider sits on the right diagonal (the right forefoot and left hind foot touching the ground) . . .

. . . and posts as the horse enters the left diagonal (its left forefoot and right hind foot about to touch the ground).

tionary; you won't have to exert your leg muscles and stand in the stirrups, but just rest your feet on the irons. The horse's motion will lift you. How high will depend upon the length and vigor of its stride. At a slow trot, you won't rise nearly as far as you will during a fast trot.

The horse drives itself forward by first one hind leg, then the other. You felt this double drive when you sat the trot. This time, when one hind leg pushes against the ground, let the reaction of that push lift you from the saddle. When that leg relaxes, sit until it pushes you up once more. This is the simplest description of posting. If it is the right hind leg that's pushing you, that means the left front hoof must also be touching the ground, and therefore you are posting on the *left diagonal*. Similarly, if it were the left hind leg you would be on the *right diagonal*. While posting, your hands should be held almost motionless because your horse won't be bobbling its head as it does while walking. Be sure not to vary the tension on the reins. It should be just enough to enable you to feel the horse's mouth, which is the amount you should always maintain when you are not actually using the reins as aids but just holding them ready for use.

You might not care on which diagonal you post, but the horse does. Horses are either right-handed or left-handed, or, more accurately, right-hind-legged or left-hind-legged. And each prefers to have its favored leg do the work of lifting the posting rider. In fact, it does a better job with that leg which is usually stronger. On a long trot, it's often advisable to switch diagonals to give the other hind leg its share of exercise. And, as some riders insist, to keep your horse from becoming lopsided. To change diagonals, simply sit for two beats instead of one. Or post for two beats, whichever you prefer—the latter method will spare both you and your horse an extra thump.

Turning during a trot is similar to turning in a walk. The same aids are used: a tighter rein on the inside of the turn, and pressure of the knee or heel, also on that side, to swing over the hindquarters. Remember that a horse always moves its body away from the pressure, either sideways, forward, or backward. In a turn, the choice of the diagonal on which to post is important, at least to the horse. While turning, its out-

An aid sometimes used in turning a horse is the leading rein. Here the right rein is held out to draw the horse's head directly to the right.

side legs must cover more distance than the inside legs, and its outside hind leg must push harder to keep its body in the turn. To compensate for the extra work this leg must perform, your horse will appreciate your letting its inside hind leg lift when you post. This means that in a right turn you post when the right hind hoof pushes against the ground—the left diagonal. It follows also that the right front foot will be off the ground, its shoulder low, and you can lean your body to the right to help you balance just as you bank a bicycle in a turn. Your shifted weight is also encouragement to the horse. In a left turn you post on the right diagonal.

As when walking, trotting in figure-eight patterns of various sizes is excellent practice in refining your posting and control, including changing diagonals. You'll soon learn that you don't have to look down at your horse's front hooves to determine

Another turning aid is the neck rein. Here the right rein is held against the neck and, to avoid the pressure, the horse will turn its head to the left.

which diagonal it's on; the movement of the shoulders will tell you. To slow your horse from a trot to a walk, tighten the reins slightly to restrain its forward motion. For a complete halt from a trot, squeeze your knees and at the same time gradually tighten the reins until the horse slows to a stop. And as it responds, gradually reduce the knee pressure. Don't squeeze hard and suddenly yank back the reins except in an emergency; sudden stops are rough on your horse's legs. Your horse should slow to a walk, or stop, facing its original direction. If it turns to one side, you'll know you must have been pulling harder on the rein on that side.

The canter is a slow gallop, actually not too much faster than the trot which is about eight miles per hour. It averages between ten and twelve miles per hour and is only about half as fast as a full gallop. In the canter the horse moves its legs differently than in the trot; its hooves don't touch the ground in diagonal pairs. Both hind hooves touch and push almost simultaneously and as they push, the front hooves lift and extend forward. For a brief moment the horse is not touching the ground but is hurtling through the air. As the hind legs double under its hindquarters in position for the next push, the front hooves strike the ground separately. The result is a three-beat rhythm; da-da-DUM, da-da-DUM. The first two beats are made by the front hooves, the last louder beat by the hind hooves. After each set of three, there is a pause; this is when all four hooves are off the ground. In the gallop, the legs move much faster. The front ones stretch farther forward; the rear ones drive with greater power but push separately. Both hind hooves don't strike the ground at exactly the same time. If you listen carefully, you can hear a four-beat count: da-da-DA-DUM.

There is no such thing as posting during the canter or gallop because the horse's entire body is in continual motion with no distinct thrusts that can lift you from the saddle. For the canter, your seat in the saddle can be the same as the one you used for walking and sitting the trots, the full seat, with your back straight and body relaxed. Hold your legs in their usual position but point your toes out and keep your heels down to allow your ankles to bend as your weight on them varies. As your horse canters, at the beginning of each stride (hind hooves pushing and front hooves off the ground) lean forward but return upright once more at the end of the stride.

It's relatively simple to make a horse canter from a trot, or gallop from a canter, because it's already moving fast. With your well-trained horse the only aids you need will be a touch of your heels and a loosening of the reins. But never "throw your reins away," always hold them so you can quickly tighten them if necessary. It's almost as easy to start a horse cantering from a walk, but make it a collected walk. Your horse may have been just plodding along, enjoying the scenery. Collect it by momentarily squeezing your knees slightly and tightening the reins; this will bring in its chin and its hind legs forward under its hindquarters so it will be more balanced. They'll also be in a better position to begin the faster gait. Be sure the local-

ity you've chosen for the canter or gallop is desirable—no holes
or rocks and not downhill. Grass or earth—not rock-hard—is
the best footing. Hold the reins somewhat shorter than you do
at the walk or trot because the faster you go, the farther forward your position will be, and not only do you want to feel
the bit continually, but you also want to be able to exert pressure on it to slow your horse should it go too fast. It would be
embarrassing, to say the least, to pull back the reins and find
you can't get them back far enough!

Lean farther forward than you did starting the walk. Use
knee pressure or press the horse's flank with your heels until it
responds, then immediately encourage it by slackening the

The pressure points in the leg aids: the knee and upper calf.

reins, moving your bridle hand forward. Whether you need to use just your knees or your heels or both, and to what degree, you'll have to determine by experiment. Certainly your aids will have to be more emphatic than when you started the trot. But don't go so far as to kick with your heels until you're sure such drastic prompting is necessary. If the horse simply starts to trot instead of canter, pull it up into a collected walk and start again. Don't post during its trot; you'll encourage it to repeat the mistake.

It may be that your horse will be too eager, taking off in a wild, extended gallop. This is a possibility because just like your pet pooch which has been kept inactive for most of the day, it enjoys the exercise of an all-out run. If this happens and catches you off-guard, you should have learned by now not to panic and scream for help, flopping all over its neck and flailing your legs. These strange antics will make it gallop even faster. Then as spectators help you off the ground, they'll blame the horse. "It ran away with you, eh?" You might even

Heel pressure against the horse's flank can be used as an aid. Right heel pressure against the flank will swing the hindquarters to the left for a right turn.

be tempted to blame it yourself if you're so angry you've lost all your horse sense. Actually the horse wasn't to blame; you were. In all your association with riding horses, it's your responsibility to control your mount, even if it's dashing madly away from something it fears. Any problems that arise, you must solve, not the horse. Even if it throws you, it's your fault; you should have known how to stay in the saddle. In an unexpected gallop, first be sure to maintain the usual seat and balance for that gait. Then pull back the reins and dig in your knees for just a few seconds. Don't shout. If you must say something, such as references to certain dubious characters in your horse's ancestry, try to say it calmly. If your horse doesn't slow down immediately, pull the reins and use your knees again with more vigor—and repeat until it responds.

In a canter, use the full seat (three-point contact—rump, hips, and lower legs). Remember to keep your weight well forward away from the hindquarters where the powerful legs are pumping like huge pistons. The withers have the least motion but a seat too near them would impose an extra burden on the less muscular forelegs which must lift and extend in perfect timing. Rest most of your weight on your thighs and through your legs to your heels, your rump riding lightly on the saddle.

In the faster gallop use the *half seat* (two-point contact—thighs and lower legs), your rump lifted so it "floats" a short distance above the saddle. Balance yourself as before by bending your hips and knees to conform to the horse's rhythm. A jockey, who rides high and crouches over the horse's neck, uses an extreme type of half seat, unnecessary for pleasure riding and quite tiring on the legs of anyone heavier than a jockey. In the half seat, since your weight is on the stirrups, the vertical motion of the horse's body is less severe, your flexing legs serving as shock absorbers.

When your horse canters or gallops, its front hooves do not touch the ground at the same time, as stated previously. One leg extends farther and its hoof touches first. If this is the left leg, the horse is said to be on a *left lead;* the right leg is a *right lead.* These leads ordinarily aren't important to a beginner on a trained horse. The lead the horse uses will be the one it prefers, depending upon whether it's right-handed (right-legged) or left-handed. To an owner or trainer, however, it is important that the horse becomes accustomed to using both and can change from one to the other voluntarily when beginning a turn. The horse on which you'll be learning the fast gaits will make this change probably without your being aware of it.

A horse cantering on a right lead places most of its weight on the right, and when making a right turn, actually banks its body to the right, leaning way over if the turn is sharp. While on this right lead, should it try a turn to the left it would be turning on its weaker side opposite to its weight and would be

While galloping, this horse is on a left lead, the left forefoot striking the ground first.

seriously unbalanced. It could fall or trip. It would be like riding a bike on a left turn while banking it to the right. You will be able to determine which lead your horse is on by watching its shoulders. With each step, the shoulder of the leading leg will rise higher. If you're tall enough to see its front hooves, the leading one will also come up higher. When you've discovered which lead your horse is cantering on, let's say it's a right lead, try a left turn and see if you can spot its instinctive change to a left lead.

Eventually you will learn how to put a horse into the lead you desire and to change its lead when cantering or galloping. This may even be necessary with a horse that must be reminded to change for an opposite turn. To start on a right lead from a collected walk, increase tension on the left rein and press with both heels, most firmly with the left one. Your heel pressure will indicate a faster gait. With its head pulled to the left, its weight shifted to the right by your left heel and leg, it will step out on its right leg because this is the most comfortable way to go.

Wait until you've had considerable experience with your horse before attempting to change leads during a full gallop. The main problem is to determine how forcefully, and with what slight variations, the aids must be used. Basically, the reins are tightened a slight amount, and heel or knee pressure is used to keep the horse moving. Then, as the leading hoof leaves the ground, the rein on the opposite side is tightened. For example: on a left lead, as the left hoof lifts, the right rein is tightened. Ordinarily this would indicate a right turn. But simultaneously the left-heel pressure is increased—not the right as in a right turn. The horse changes to a right lead, just as it would if it were preparing actually to turn right. But before it turns, slacken the right rein and it will continue straight ahead on the new lead. Some horses are so well-trained and know their riders so intimately that just leaning over the shoulder is enough to make them change to the lead on that side.

When you've mastered the fast gaits and can use the aids instinctively, you are on your way to becoming an accomplished horseman or horsewoman. Don't listen to criticism from would-be friends; each might have a different way of doing things, not always suited to you. Even riding instructors advise different techniques. With experience you'll be able to determine which are the best for you and your horse. Frequently you will compromise. If you are having difficulties, however, depend only on your instructor to help you solve them. Of course, you may be making mistakes of which you're not aware; occasionally have a friend with a home-movie camera shoot a film of you. Watching it, you'll quickly be able to spot errors in your seat, and the positions of your arms, legs, etc. But try to correct them only if you feel it will improve your horse's performance, not your appearance. Your horse's performance is the true evaluation of your horsemanship.

A Thoroughbred racer out for some exercise. Note the short stirrups to facilitate the jockey's very high half seat when the horse is running.

8. Over the Bars

Just as you were impatient to trot, canter, and gallop, after you've practiced these gaits for a while you will be anxious to try jumping. But attempting too soon will be inviting trouble. Your instructor is the only one to judge when you're ready, and he or she will tell you. Then you'll be jumping under adequate supervision. There's no doubt that it will be one of the most thrilling riding adventures you'll ever have, but it involves a certain risk. Obviously, a spill from a jump can have regrettable results. To be sure of avoiding one, you must follow certain rules.

A horse jumping without a rider never falls; the exceptions are extremely rare. It glides over a barrier with the greatest of ease. The lesson to be learned from this is that during the actual jump, from take-off to landing, you should remain as inconspicuous as possible; you are just excess baggage. You must do nothing to restrict the horse's natural jumping ability. You will hear riders say that you must "lift" your horse over the barrier; perhaps if you feel that you are doing so—although actually doing little—you'll at least have a positive mental attitude. The horse is really the only one doing the lifting. Your principal job is to remain balanced with the horse during the jump, which isn't difficult if you've already learned to balance yourself on the half seat while galloping. The variations for the jump are slight. You use your aids only to direct it toward the barrier and encourage it if necessary. Later you might have to help a horse time its jump, but this won't be true with the horse assigned to you for your lessons.

Most important, your experience in the fast gaits will have increased your confidence which your horse will sense and, in return, will be confident in you. If you're hesitant, a trifle scared, your horse might balk at the last second, taking you by surprise. Then there's a possibility you'll make the jump without your horse!

There are few sights more exhilarating and exciting than that of a magnificent horse gracefully clearing a high barrier. It is a symphony of perfect muscular co-ordination and timing, every part of its body co-operating in the tremendous effort. Its performance is another of nature's marvels, too; no other animal of its size or weight can jump half as high or as far, or with such precision.

When approaching a barrier, a reliable jumper certainly shows an indication of intelligence that is more than simple in-

Trotting over ground poles help to prepare a horse for jumping.

stinct. During this approach in a canter or gallop, it estimates the distance it must cover, the height it must jump and, if it can see beyond the barrier as it gets close to it, how far it must jump. Sometimes it will slow its gait slightly at the barrier to select the best distance from it for a take-off, just as a track athlete sometimes takes a couple of shorter steps before launching himself upward for a high jump. For a broad jump, the horse selects a spot farther from the barrier.

In its last stride, all pertinent factors evaluated, it prepares to spring. It lowers its hindquarters and brings its hind legs farther under its body. As they push forward, the forelegs push up to lift the withers until its body is correctly angled upward to clear the barrier. At the same time, it throws its head forward, neck outstretched, to add to its momentum. As it crosses over the barrier, its forelegs are folded up, the hind legs drawn back, ready to restore the body's balance as soon as the forelegs touch. The balancing effect of its head is important to a jumping horse. In a jump for distance rather than height, such as across a wide stream, it will keep its head extended when its front hooves touch the far bank. Then, when the hind hooves touch just behind the front ones, the weight of the head and neck, swinging down from the shoulders which act as a fulcrum, helps to lift the hindquarters, and maintain the balance without lessening the forward momentum.

During the landing the horse changes leads. Both front hooves don't touch the ground at the same time. If the horse entered the jump from a right lead, it will almost always land the same way—right hoof first. The shock of the landing can be as much as eight times the horse's weight, but it is not born entirely by the right leg; it is shared by the left leg, its hoof touching immediately after the right one. And since this left leg must stretch out farther than the right to sustain the weight as the horse continues forward, it becomes the leading leg; the horse now canters or gallops from the barrier on a left lead. However, if after leaving the barrier you signal for a right turn, the horse can change back to a right lead in a single stride.

The jumper is also frequently called a *hunter* because its practical use is in English-style fox hunting when it must gallop over hill and dale and en route jump unexpected stone walls, brooks, and fences. In preparing for a jump, some hunters show better judgment than others, of course, but the one chosen for your training should be sufficiently reliable to allow you to concentrate on your own problems almost exclusively. Your barrier will have bars to which additional ones can be added to increase its height. And it probably will have wings, used to persuade an inexperienced horse to take the jump instead of *running out* (circling around the barrier), which to even this "unintelligent" animal seems the logical way to get past it. Your horse won't need these wings, but they might help you line up for a straight approach.

Making a straight approach is most important. Since a horse has poor depth perception even under ideal conditions, approaching a barrier at an angle might seriously handicap its judgment of height and distance. Some horses like to approach any barrier at a full gallop, apparently believing that maximum speed is always essential to clear it; the result may be a take-off unnecessarily far from it. Of course, an exceptionally

This horse is "running out"—it has refused to jump the bars.

extended (spread) barrier does require a fast approach to provide momentum for the longer jump. Others prefer to trot up,
hesitate for a moment while they reassess the situation, then
jump from almost a standstill. These are problems you will
eventually meet, and you will learn to cope with them by
using the needed restraint or urging as the case may be. For
your first jump you will probably start a fair distance from the
barrier so you'll have time to get settled properly. But realize
that not only is full-speed seldom necessary; neither is a
hundred-yard start. To clear a six-foot barrier, a good hunter
needs only a half-dozen strides.

The last three strides are the most important ones; during
them your horse will make its final preparations to jump. Take
the half seat if you approached the barrier in a trot or canter;
you'll already be in it if you approached in a gallop. Resting
your weight on your ankles and balancing yourself with your
thighs tight against the saddle, incline your torso forward so it
is in line with the path the horse's body will take as it lifts to
clear the barrier. As the horse jumps, in order to jump with it—
not behind it—you will have to lean farther forward and rise in
a higher half seat. While crossing the barrier, your torso will
be almost parallel with the ground. Then, in preparation for
landing, gradually straighten and resume the normal half seat.
During the different stages of the jump, your sense of balance
actually will tell you how far to lean forward.

Your legs should function like the coil-spring suspension on a
car. A moment before landing, be prepared to absorb the shock
with your knees and ankles. As soon as you land, you'll be
tempted to flop back into the saddle. If you do, you might accidentally draw back the reins, also, and the horse won't know
what to do with its hind hooves because its front hooves
haven't given them enough room to land. Lower your body
gently as you canter away from the barrier. After a jump, unless your instructor has other plans for you, stop after continuing a dozen yards or so and give your horse a few pats and
kind words to show it you're pleased, especially if it still hasn't
decided you're worth considering a friend.

Things can happen at the moment of jump that may rattle a
beginner. Suppose your horse, a usually reliable jumper, de-

The hunter is clearing the jump and is about to draw up its hind legs. Note the inclination of the rider's body.

The hunter landed on a right lead, but now the left leg has stretched farther forward to help absorb the shock of the landing, and the horse will continue on a left lead.

cides abruptly to refuse the jump and stop, or to swerve and run out! The reason may be a blowing piece of paper, or sudden distrust in your horsemanship. Unprepared for such an emergency and up in the half seat, you'll have difficulty keeping your balance and might topple. Also it's common for a horse momentarily to check its stride, or shorten it, in order to choose its take-off spot. Again, as a beginner, you're facing trouble. What usually happens is that as it checks, you rock forward over its neck and you're "ahead of the horse," then when it jumps, its thrust out from under you will bang you back down on the saddle. It's a kind of "equine whiplash," and unpleasant for the horse as well as for you. But all these unforeseen situations can be made quite harmless by a slight variation in your seat, which might not look as professional to spectators but will serve until you acquire more experience. During those last three strides, take the full seat down on the saddle, and push your rump against the cantle. In this position you're anchored and difficult to dislodge no matter what happens. Incline your torso in the direction of "flight." Then when the horse jumps your body will be aligned with its thrust which will lift you forward out of the saddle into the high half seat previously described.

What to do with your reins during a jump is vitally important. Or, that is, what you DON'T do with them. They must not restrain your horse in any way. During the entire jump a skillful rider can hold them so delicately that he or she can just feel the horse's mouth; this is difficult because of the extreme changes in position of the horse's head. During your approach, it's advisable to adjust your reins so you can hold your hands farther back than during the normal canter or gallop. Remember that when your horse jumps, it extends its neck. As you rise higher than the half seat and lean farther forward at the jump, also extend your hands to the horse's withers; this should give you enough slack rein. If it doesn't, let the reins slip through your fingers. As a beginner, you are permitted to lean on the withers to help your balance, and even grab a handful of mane if necessary.

No reins at all are preferable to tight ones. A horse can jump beautifully without them. If you ever happen to find yourself in the situation previously described, where your horse's sudden hesitation just before the jump throws you forward, then backward, release the reins. Don't freeze to them and haul them back with you. A spill isn't as dangerous as having the horse fall on you, which it might do if it doesn't have sufficient poise to overcome its confusion and continue to a co-ordinated landing. This warning should in no way discourage you from jumping; it is intended simply to alert you to what can be one of the most serious mistakes you can make as a rider, so you can avoid it.

Most of your early jumping practice will be over barriers with bars. Each bar rests on supports on the far sides of the upright poles so that if your jumper kicks the top one (not its

This Quarter Horse is a hunter, too. The rider's position is horizontal due to extreme speed in the approach, a take-off far from the bars, and the vigor of the jump. (American Quarter Horse Association.)

fault but perhaps because you tightened the reins), it will fall free. Often the bars are padded to protect the horse's shins. Old car tires, hung in strategic places, aren't very decorative but they're efficient bumpers. To increase the height of the barrier, one or more bars are added; a single bar isn't moved up as in the high jump or pole vault at a track meet. The reason is that one thin bar on two thin poles is too difficult for a horse to see when it must judge distance and height on its approach. Should you have your own horse some day, for the same reason don't ask it to jump a bare two-by-four resting on a couple of wooden horses or stumps; at least drape a blanket over the pole or put some brush in front of it to make it more visible.

During your training you may also be asked to jump a course consisting of several barriers in succession. In the training of the hunters themselves, schools often use barriers called *cavalletti*, developed by the Italian riding masters. Each consists of two X-shaped wooden supports standing about ten feet apart with a pole resting in the top V of each of the Xs. Cavalletti have advantages over the bars. They're easily portable; to increase height, they can be placed one on top of the other. And a number of them placed one behind the other form a broader barrier for distance jumping. Also, since they require no vertical poles, they more nearly resemble natural obstacles.

If you want to take your own hunter cross-country, it's wise first to acquaint the horse with barriers it won't find in the paddock, so it won't hesitate at one because it doesn't look familiar. Use piles of brush, logs, hay, a neighbor's stone wall. Vary their size and shape. Construct a water jump about a foot deep and extending five feet, its edges sloping, not vertical, to protect the horse's legs should it make a mistake. Should your horse decide to wade across it instead of jumping it, put a log or some brush along the front edge. A distance jump is essentially the same as a high jump as far as both you and the horse are concerned; it still must jump high enough so its trajectory will carry it to the other side, and you're along just for the ride.

Most hunters time their jumps and choose their points of take-off with no help from their riders. They have better judgment, which isn't surprising; they do the actual jumping. But some horses are trained not to jump until signaled by the rider. Before jumping a strange hunter, be sure to ask its owner or handler if it needs any help. If so, the timing will be up to you, but you will easily handle it if you already know how to "jump with your horse."

With experience you will soon become a polished rider over

For cross-country trips, give your horse experience in jumping new barriers. This one resembles a fence. But don't take chances like this young rider; wear a helmet. (American Saddle Horse Breeders Association.)

the hurdles and realize how easy it is, not difficult as you supposed at the beginning. For example, you will find it unnecessary to lean against your horse's withers as it clears the bars; with your body in perfect balance, your hands will move with the horse's head on a straight line between your elbows and the bit. And you will understand what riders mean when they say, "Throw your heart over the fence and your horse will follow it." Approach every jump with determination and confidence, and your horse won't disappoint you.

SECTION III
Your Own Horse or Pony

9. Choosing the Right One

Buying a horse or pony isn't as simple as stepping into an automobile showroom, writing a check and driving off in a new car, but there are interesting similarities. Your choice depends on how much you can afford to pay, of course, also its brand (or breed) name, and how you plan to use it. Do you want to learn on it, will you be content to just loaf along, or do you want high performance? If you recently obtained your driver's license in a Volkswagen with an automatic transmission, you're not yet ready for a souped-up four-on-the-floor Maserati. Similarly, if you're still just a student horseman, you'll probably find the average Thoroughbred too hot to handle.

If the vehicle you're considering is secondhand, which all horses really are except for one you might rear from a foal, did its previous owner treat it with care, or abuse it? The flaws in a horse can be mental as well as physical, not as easy to spot as a dented fender or a rust spot. For example: a horse that has hit its shins too many times while carrying students over the bars may have been ruined as a hunter; you won't know until you've seen it try a jump. Sometimes a good hunter, ridden by someone who is unfamiliar with how it must be handled, will run right through the bars, and thereafter might be difficult to convince that it was all a mistake.

Just as you should ask an expert mechanic to check a used car before you buy it, you'll be wise to get the opinion of an experienced horseman—not someone who just says he or she knows horses, but a rider who you know is definitely an expert. Then you'll obtain a reliable opinion of the horse's points and conformation, and the test ride will reveal any physical or emotional hang-ups. You'll probably have to pay for the advice, but it will be a worthwhile investment. Finally, make another investment; hire a vet to check the horse's health.

If you're not buying from a reputable dealer, who would like you to return someday and do business with him again, you'd better know about "horse trading." It's a kind of bargaining game that has been practiced ever since the horse first returned to America. The seller will describe his horse to you in the most glowing terms. He would like you to believe it is heaven's gift to horsemen, it can do anything, the most perfect specimen that has ever been bred. If you think it's sway-back

This horse isn't going to bite; it just wants attention. But you will want a horse that's more than just friendly; it must be sound and capable of reasonable performance.

and knock-kneed, this simply means you don't know horseflesh. It's up to you and your hired adviser to show him you're smarter than you look. He expects it and won't be hostile. It's all part of the game. I know of one case where a naïve shopper accepted everything the seller said without question; he was so surprised and confused that he suffered pangs of conscience and refused to sell her the horse! Also you'll have to do some dickering over the final price. If you're not a shrewd bargainer, you'd better get help from someone who is. Your horse evaluator should know how to handle this problem, too. And when the price is finally set, ask the seller to throw in a used saddle and bridle as part of the deal. Don't be too embarrassed to ask; even car dealers will gladly add whitewall tires or an air conditioner to clinch a sale.

New Englanders are famous for their trading. There's a story about a horseman from Connecticut who went to a small breeder in Maine to buy a Morgan. Outside the stable he met the owner. "Got any horses?" he asked casually. "Nope," the man answered. Of course the visitor could hear the horses in the stable and could even see a number of them in the pasture. "I thought I heard one," he said. "Maybe I have one," the owner replied, not showing much interest. "For sale?" The answer was another "Nope." Then, as the horseman turned to walk away, the owner added, "But you can look at it if you've a mind to." This verbal sparring was the beginning of the trading session. Neither contestant wanted to appear too anxious; it would put him at a disadvantage. The main event was hectic at times, lasted the better part of two days, but both men were winners. The breeder got a good price and my friend took home a fine bay Morgan.

It's not difficult to find horses for sale. They're advertised in the classified sections of daily newspapers, as well as in such magazines as the weekly *Chronicle of the Horse* (Berryville, Virginia 22611) and the monthly *Western Horseman* (3850 North Nevada Avenue, Colorado Springs, Colorado 80933). Your riding instructor, various riding academies listed in your phone book, saddlery shops, and horse vets will be able to help. Don't rely on a horse auction; not only do you need a practiced eye to spot decent horseflesh, but there's seldom an

opportunity for a close inspection of the merchandise. Prices
often are lower in parts of the country where the supply ex-
ceeds the demand and trading is brisk. Sometimes you can
save considerably by canvassing this horse country, finding a
likely prospect, then hiring a local unbiased horse expert and
vet to help you make the final decision. You can tow your
purchase home in a rented trailer. In the northern states beginning in late autumn, prices are often less than in spring or summer. Sales are slow because there's not as much riding activity
during the winter, and owners can reduce their prices and still
make a larger profit than they would in spring after the expense of stabling and feeding their horses during the slow
months.

For a reasonably respectable and sound pleasure horse, expect to pay a minimum of about $750. It won't win any beauty
prizes, but neither will it be some poor browbeaten nag, and
its amble and three faster gaits should provide you with many
enjoyable hours on the bridle paths and trails. If you're still

Paints *make excellent and attractive riding horses, but a cute colt
or filly needs training and may be too much for a beginner to
handle.* (American Paint Horse Association.)

learning to ride, you'd better pay a higher price for one that's had considerable training. The horseman's proverb mentioned in a previous chapter still applies: "A green horse and a green rider are a poor color combination." If you're green, be sure your horse isn't. It should know more about riding than you do. It can even make an excellent teacher, correcting your mistakes. I remember a gelding named Demon (misnamed by the small son of its previous owner, who was fascinated by rodeos) that was a great help in training young riders. When given the wrong aids, or given them improperly, it would refuse to move; if already moving, it would halt in its tracks and had to be started all over again.

Seldom will you find a good horse for sale for less than the price mentioned above unless you buy from a personal friend or from a young rider who must go back to school. The crossbreds or *grade* horses—having no pedigree—are the least expensive. Often they are the result of accidental mating, such as when a pedigreed stallion jumps a fence and finds a mare of undetermined ancestry. The breeder is anxious to get rid of them, often without the benefit of much training, however. That's up to the buyer, who might be the operator of a dude ranch, a trail-riding outfit, or a riding school. Or even you, if you feel you're qualified to train a green horse. The horse on which you took your first lessons was probably a grade, although your instructor might have stretched a point and called it an Arab or a Morgan, depending on which ancestor it resembled most. Grades may be cheaper, not as handsome, but are not necessarily inferior. As in the canine world, the "mongrels" are often the healthiest, most durable, and most intelligent. Figure—named after its ridiculous figure—founder of the Morgan breed, was an unknown crossbred.

Geldings are cheaper, especially when aged, because they have no breeding potential. One of them might be your best choice. Generally they're easier to handle than stallions and have quieter temperaments. Very few of them are fighters, but any stallion will accept another's challenge to fight over a mare. If you're riding a gelding and meet a mare that wants to breed, your horse won't show much interest. But if you're on a stallion, you may be in for a spot of trouble, as will the rider of the mare. Mares are smaller, more agile, and frequently more sensitive and intelligent, but unplanned motherhood can cause problems you may not have anticipated, only one of which is expense.

Horses that have passed their prime and have been retired from active duty, anything from playing polo to roping cattle at a rodeo, have lower price tags. Don't overlook one if it's still physically sound. They're well trained and responsive, used to riders, easy to handle, and have a generous supply of horse sense. They often make fine pleasure horses. Don't pass up a horse because you think it's too old. A gelding of fifteen years or more, regarded by its owner as just a useless "hayburner" not earning its board and keep, may be a real bargain. It still has enough left to make a good saddle horse until it's over twenty. Be cautious about buying a pure Thoroughbred. Majestic and powerful, it's the Rolls-Royce of the horse world. In capable hands it can do just about anything well, including jumping. If you decide you must own one, first be sure you have those capable hands.

A Standardbred, rejected because it wasn't fast enough on the track, can be bought at a reasonable price. It can become a good pleasure horse, especially for trail riding. Its modern specialized use in trotting and pacing races conceals its overall ability. Its New England ancestors lived close to their owners, were used for many family chores in addition to carrying riders, and became man-wise. Today's Standardbred has lost little of this heritage. It has a quieter temperament than the Thoroughbred, is eager to respond to its rider, and easily learns gaits other than its natural trot and pace. It also makes a good hunter. Its main disadvantage is that it must be trained as a saddle horse since most of its experience has been in a sulky harness. This means you must hire a trainer, an added expense unless you can do the job yourself.

When you find a horse that looks good to you, it's time to find out how good it looks to your expert horseman. First, he'll judge its conformation which, explained simply, means all its parts and how they're put together. Standards differ among the various registered breeds, but there are some points all horses should have for good average performance. Even in these you

Thoroughbreds *can become good saddle horses if they can forget they were bred for high-speed racing.*

will have to compromise to some degree if your budget is limited. And there are exceptions to every rule. You may have to settle for some bad points, but be sure they're outweighed by the good ones.

The head should not be a *hammerhead*, too large and heavy; it will affect the horse's balance, putting too much weight up front. The forehead should be broad, indicating good brain capacity. The eyes mirror the horse's disposition, which will never change; the vet will determine how healthy they are, but to the horseman they reflect the horse's intelligence, poise, *savoir-faire*, and friendliness to strangers. The neck should be long rather than short; a short neck usually means a choppy gait and requires a heavy hand on the reins. So does a *bull neck*, one that's too thick and muscled. A horse with a *ewe neck*, wider at the top than at the bottom, is a star gazer, holding its head high, and is not considered safe to jump.

The shoulders ideally should slope forward at an angle of about 45 degrees; if the slope is almost vertical, it will restrict the movements of the forelegs. The chest should be deep to show adequate lung capacity, and the back short and straight with prominent withers to hold back the saddle. The legs and feet are very important. Knock-knees, pigeon-toes, splayfeet that toe out, bowlegs, cannon bones that are too long, inhibit the horse and cause increased strain on the legs when it tries to use them normally; these conditions can lead to lameness or worse. The feet should be large so that the portion of the horse's weight each must carry is distributed over a wide area. When the horseman lifts a foot to examine the hoof, the horse should permit it without making a fuss. The hoof should be wider at the bottom than at the coronet, have a concave sole with a sizable, flexible frog, and when on the ground the foot should slope forward at a 45 degree angle.

Next, your "pro" will test ride the horse to check its performance and handling. It should stand quietly while being mounted, then move out with normal persuasion, and be able and willing to walk quietly, trot, and canter. And jump, if that is one of your requirements. The expert will be able to tell you not only how well it performs these maneuvers, but also how comfortable it is to ride in the gaits, and with how much vigor

This Paint *performs like a* Quarter Horse. *Discarded rodeo horses, if sound, can settle down to lives of pleasure riding.* (American Paint Horse Association.)

you will have to use the aids. Maybe it has a hard mouth, which means you'll have to be heavy-handed with the reins to make it respond. Maybe it's too easily excited. Suggest that the rider wear a brightly colored slicker to determine the horse's reaction to it, if any. Also, the horse might be ridden out on the highway to see if it's spooked by a passing car. Is it sure-footed or inclined to stumble? After the rider has dismounted, does it stand patiently waiting? Finally, find out what the horse thinks of you, since you're the one who will have to live with it. Does it react just as calmly and willingly to you as it did to the expert, or was it charmed by his confidence and ability and now resents the intrusion of someone lacking the same

If you want a horse for show-hunting or trail-riding competition, have an expert test it for sure-footedness and its ability to jump natural barriers. (Meredith Manor School of Horsemanship.)

qualities? Or maybe it just plain dislikes you. It's entitled to its opinion; after all, you don't like everyone you meet, either. You may hide your dislike; a horse doesn't.

The vet will get right down to the nitty-gritty, spotting flaws that might not be obvious to the horseman. He'll tell you how *sound* (healthy, in horse talk) the horse is. He'll look for many symptoms. The horse may be *wind-broken,* usually the result of a previous attack of flu. The symptom is a rushing sound when the breath is inhaled after hard exercise such as a gallop, and such a horse should be neither galloped for long periods nor jumped. *Thrush* is a disease of the frog in the foot, sometimes destroying the frog completely; the vet can detect it in its early stages. A hip that has been *knocked down* is one that has sustained a slight fracture almost invisible externally. A *cracked toe* is a fracture of the front wall of the hoof. A crack on the side of the wall, caused by a shoe nail incorrectly placed in a hoof that's too brittle, can lead to lameness. An enlarged *sesamoid* eventually causes incurable lameness; it is the hardening of the cartilage surrounding the sesamoid bones of the fetlock joint, restricting the action of the tendons. Another serious ailment is a *bowed tendon,* caused by the excessive stress imposed on the tendon near the cannon when the horse is repeatedly required to gallop from a standing start, or by similar extreme exertion. Thoroughbreds and Quarter Horses are prone to it. Still another, often serious, is a *ringbone,* a hard growth around one of the pastern bones, caused by a sprain or accidental blow. A *withers fistula* is first a swelling, then a large abscess, on the withers, resulting in stiffness of the shoulders. A *poll evil* is similar but not as serious. Both are caused by an injury.

The vet doesn't have to conduct his examination on the same day as your qualified horseman. It's more convenient and costs less of the vet's valuable time if he does his job after the horse is in your stable. And this is possible if the seller agrees to give you a trial period of perhaps two weeks or ten days. He might charge an extra fee for the privilege, but you'll be saving money on the vet's bill. Also, the fact that he agrees to such an arrangement will show that he's confident you won't find anything seriously wrong with the merchandise. And during that trial period you'll be able to learn about the horse's stable behavior.

It's good business practice to have all terms of the sale in writing; don't settle for a verbal agreement and a handshake. Unfortunately, perhaps, this is true even when you're dealing with a friend. State all the terms clearly—a complete description of the horse including its sex, name, and color; the seller's declaration of its age and soundness, and his guarantee that he's the owner; any accessories he's including in the sale; the purchase price, amount of down payment, fee for the trial period, its duration, the fact that your final decision to purchase will depend upon your vet's opinion; and that should you decide not to purchase the horse, your total indebtedness to him will be only the fee for the trial period. Such a contract, dated and signed by both parties, will protect him as well as you.

Any pedigree papers, if the horse is a purebred, should be transferred to you on the final date of sale.

Now you have a horse of your own and your dream has come true. Take good care of it and be kind to it; its health and happiness depend entirely on you. In return, it will reward you with many pleasant hours in the saddle. You'll discover all its imperfections, but ride with them. Adapt to them by becoming a better horseman. Nothing in the world is perfect. Someday, after you've saved enough money, you might buy a pedigreed Arabian. Then you'll be surprised to discover that it has imperfections, too. After you've become a veteran horseman, you'll often think of the day you bought your first horse; you'll remember it as one of the happiest days of your life.

10. Its New Home

Now that you own a horse, your problem is where to keep it. It's one you certainly were aware of, and perhaps even solved, before you went shopping for the new addition to your family. You probably prefer to keep it at home. Having it in your back yard where you can spend as much time with it as possible, attending to its needs, is one of the joys of owning a horse. And it has other advantages besides convenience; your personal attention will make the horse realize its dependence upon you as its lord and master. But maybe you don't have enough room on your property for one; it needs about an acre. Maybe the local zoning laws exclude horses. Or maybe you don't yet have adequate facilities for it. A solution might be to find a friendly horse owner not too far away who will keep it for you if you add a stall for your horse and be responsible for its care. As a last resort you can always board it at a large stable; this might be the school where you learned to ride. Such stables almost always have an empty stall or two they're happy to rent for a price. Some stables specialize in boarding horses.

A boarding stable might not be listed by that name in your phone book, but you can find one by asking your riding instructor or other horsemen. Its rates vary according to how much service you require and are lowest, of course, in rural areas. If all you want to do is fetch your horse, tack it up, go for a ride and then return it, letting the stable hands do the rest of the work, this de luxe service can cost as much as $250 monthly. But for "rough board," where the stable provides the stall, feed, and bedding, and you take care of the tack, grooming, exercising, vet, and blacksmith fees, the cost can be as low as $125 a month, even in suburbia. The Kentucky Stables in Harrison, New York, a short distance north of New York City, charges $150 a month and offers a "box stall" which is larger than the usual "standing stall" and allows the horse more freedom. In many boarding stables, even with rough board you won't have to pay for exercising and grooming; there are young riders who spend their free time at the stable and are so fond of horses they will gladly do these chores for you in return for the opportunity to ride yours.

It's best to look over a boarding stable carefully before deciding to entrust your horse to it. Ideally, it should offer the use of the adjacent countryside and riding trails, also a riding ring for jumping and competitive riding. Box stalls are preferable to the standing type, as previously mentioned. They should

In many boarding stables, young riders who love horses will exercise and groom yours just for the opportunity to ride it.

be well ventilated and drained, with a floor that's neither too hard nor too soft. A hard floor such as concrete, even when covered with a layer of asphalt, can hurt the feet of a horse that must stand on it most of the time. And asphalt is slippery when wet. This is also true of a wooden floor. One of soft earth retains moisture, except in very dry parts of the country, and causes a kind of equine athlete's foot called *thrush* which attacks the frog. A clay floor is best; it acts almost like kitty litter.

Look for protruding nails, wire, or other objects on which a horse can injure itself. You may not find them often, but surprisingly a number of stable owners overlook them. Cleanliness is always important, not only in the stalls but also the water buckets and feed boxes. Notice whether the horses already boarding there are happy to see one of the stable hands when he approaches. Finally, ask your vet if he recommends the stable, and if it suffers from an annual attack of a disease such as winter flu. Also ask him what immunizing inoculations he recommends for your horse. Whether or not you decide to use a boarding stable, it's wise to know the location of a good one; it will come in handy when you have to go away on a vacation, or for some reason can't give your horse all the attention it needs.

With your horse at home, a well-equipped stable is ideal but not necessary. Many horses live outdoors all year, like their wild ancestors, and don't suffer unusual hardship. In fact, they're often healthier. Basically, all you need is a corral so the horse won't wander off. One 50′×100′ is adequate. A 4-foot fence is high enough, unless your horse discovers it can jump without you on its back. And it should be constructed of rails with firmly planted posts, or of chain link, strong enough so that your horse can't push it down when it's playful. The rails must be treated with creosote to withstand the weather and so the horse won't chew them. Place them close together, or just slightly apart so the horse can't catch its head between them, which might be fatal. If the chain-link fence extends down into the ground, a hoof or leg can't get caught under it. The gate must have a latch the horse can't possibly open; if there's a way it can open the latch, it will find it. Ask any old-time

Your horse will enjoy a pasture with tender grass, but it will be content with just a paddock and frequent exercise and good feed.

horseman. And there should be a means of holding the gate fully open. There's nothing more discouraging to both horse and rider than approaching a gateway and finding the gate swinging shut.

Any rocks in the corral must be removed to protect the horse's feet. The ground shouldn't be too hard for the same reason. Also, hard ground becomes slippery when wet. And the corral must be located in an area of good drainage where water won't collect in pools. In the wild, a horse stands under a tree for protection from the hot sun, a cold winter wind, or a driving sleet storm. In your corral provide similar shelter with an open shed or lean-to, its back facing the prevailing winds. The two prime necessities of life you must provide for your horse are plenty of fresh water and good feed. An old bathtub makes a good watering trough; if you think its presence de-

tracts from the charm of your landscape, paint it green or dec-
orate it with decals or horse-talk graffiti. Outside the corral, of
course, you'll need an area in which you can ride, jump, and
give your horse a change of scenery.

If you decide to build your own stable, the project is
simplified if you have a barn or unused garage that can be converted. With a garage, if it has a concrete floor, first remove it.
Plan the stall in a spot that has good ventilation, such as a real
window. Remove the glass and cover the frame with heavy
wire mesh. A glass window is dangerous; your horse might
break it and cut itself. A box stall of 10'×10' is a minimum
size; 12'×12' is better. In fact, you can give your horse the
entire barn or garage in which to wander around, but the most
obvious disadvantage of your generosity would be you'd have
a much larger area to keep clean. Don't locate the stall where
the ceiling is low; a minimum of 10-feet headroom is necessary
so your horse won't hit its head when it rears. Wooden walls,
treated with creosote, should be at least 7 feet high so the
horse won't be tempted to reach the top with its hooves.

The door, at least 5 feet wide so that you and the horse can
walk through it side-by-side without squeezing, should open
outward. You might prefer the Dutch type, its upper and
lower sections swinging separately. The upper section can be
opened for cross-ventilation if the ceiling and walls seal the
top of the stall. This also lets the horse watch what's going on
outside while the closed lower section keeps it from leaving
the stall. Another popular stall door, used by many boarding
stables and schools, isn't divided into two sections like the
Dutch type but instead has a top half made of vertical bars.
This provides ventilation but doesn't let the horse stick out its
head. Its advantage is it prevents nipping, which can happen
when a visitor unfamiliar with horses extends a friendly hand
for a pat and the horse, expecting a lump of sugar, misin-
terprets the gesture.

Heat is unnecessary in a stable. A well-fed horse generates
sufficient body heat to keep out the winter cold. Neither does
it need artificial lighting; it can see in the dark. But you, with
your inferior eyesight, need electric lights (150 watts each is
about right) to see while working in the stall and stable. Keep

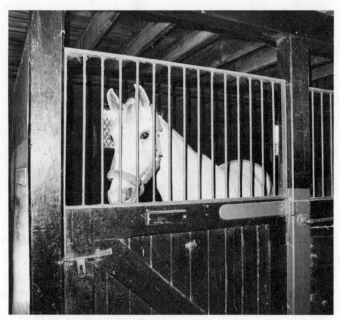

A common stall door has bars at the top to keep a horse from nipping a stranger when it expects a piece of sugar.

all bulbs and electric wires out of your horse's reach. Mount the water bucket and the feed box inside the front of the stall, not in the rear where to reach it you must push past the horse's hindquarters and risk an affectionate kick. Have cross-ties in the stall, or outside in better light if more convenient. These are two ropes or chains extending from opposite walls at the horse's eye level that can be snapped to its halter. They are used to steady it while it is being groomed, shoed, or treated by the vet. The ties should be rather tight; your horse might catch its leg in one that's too loose. You can also build a tack room next to the stall, or keep your tack in some other handy place in the barn or garage where it can be locked away from prying hands. Stealing horses isn't as popular as it was in the Old West; today it's almost impossible to resell them. But tack has been known to disappear mysteriously.

Building your own complete stable might seem like a large investment at first, but it isn't more expensive than keeping

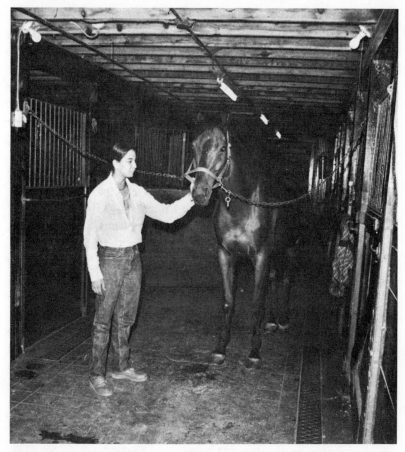

Crossties are necessary to hold your horse's head steady when you're grooming its coat, or when it's being treated by the vet or farrier.

your horse in a boarding stable when the initial cost is amortized over the years. Choose a site with good drainage. A simple design is a small building about 20′×12′ with a roof that slants from 14 feet in front (one of the long sides) to 10 feet in the rear. This slant helps shed the snow, also the water when it melts. Have the roof project about 5 feet over the front of the building to shade it and to protect it from the rain and snow. This will be sufficient if the back faces the prevailing winds in your area. If the roof also projects 2 or 3 feet in the rear, the water runoff will not be close to the building. With an interior wall, divide the building into two rooms, one 12'×12' and the other 8'×12'. The larger one will be the stall, the smaller one your tack room.

A 5×7-foot Dutch door can be installed in the front center of the stall so when its top section is open, your horse can look out at the outside world. But at night you will want to close this section, so place a screened window near the door. This, plus another screened window in the rear of the stall, will provide ventilation. Your tack room will need a glass window or two and a solid door, plus a heater. An electric heater is the easiest to install. Just plug it in. But a small bottle-gas radiator such as the one I use made by Coleman, famous for its stoves and lanterns, is less expensive to operate and even more satisfactory because it distributes heat by means of circulating air currents rather than by radiation.

You can build this simple stable yourself from precut materials. I have used those supplied by the Ward Cabin Company, Box 72, Bangor, Maine 04730. The walls are made of bug-resistant white cedar logs, without bark, half round on the outside for an attractive rustic appearance, and flat on the inside to resemble horizontal paneling. Since they are tongue-and-groove and precut to size, they are easy to assemble. The company furnishes everything including the roof, doors, windows, and hardware—even nails and caulking compound to seal the crevices between the logs. When you submit your rough plan, the company will send you an accurate architectural drawing for your approval and tell you the exact price. All the material will be shipped by truck, the cost depending upon the distance. There are a number of lumber companies scattered across the country that have similar operations. For a precut stable of this size, the Ward Cabin Company currently charges about $2,500. Assemble it yourself.

Your horse will need plenty of water, and since you'll soon get tired of hauling it in buckets from your house, run a pipe from your water supply to the stable. If you're in a part of the country where the bottom drops out of the thermometer in winter, be sure the pipe is buried at least 3 feet underground (below the frost line) so the water in it won't freeze. Install the faucet on the inner side wall of the stable a few feet off the ground. If you have only a stall and tack room as in the small stable just mentioned, put the faucet in the tack room where it also will be sheltered from the cold. You can run a plastic hose out the window to fill an outside trough if you decide to have one, and to bathe your horse in summer. Keep the grain for feed in a couple of plastic garbage cans with tops that can be clamped tight so marauding critters such as rats can't get at it. If you don't have a large stable with extra storage space, you'll also need a small outside shed in which to keep your horse's hay and straw bedding for the stall. Place them on a slightly elevated platform so the air can circulate beneath them and prevent dampness and mold.

A rubber-fiber water bucket can be used in the stall. Don't hang it on a hook; when the bucket is removed for cleaning or a refill, the bare hook is a threat to your horse. A shelf is best, with the bucket placed in a hole in the shelf to anchor it so the horse can't knock it over. A similar feed tub can be used for grain. Use an elevated trough, box, or bin for hay, or a special hay net. It isn't advisable to place the grain or hay on the floor; it can become soiled, wet, and usually your horse will eat some earth and straw along with its feed. For work around the stable, you'll need a pitchfork for the hay, a rake for the straw, a broom for tidying up, and a wheelbarrow, plus a box of assorted carpenter's tools for odd jobs. Your horse will need a stable blanket if you shear off some or all of its natural heavy winter coat, and a halter for wear around the stable. The halter is a kind of abbreviated bridle without a bit; and is handy to grab hold of and hold onto when you want to lead your horse out of its stall. In an emergency you can improvise a halter by throwing a rope noose (not a slipknot) around the horse's neck and looping the rope around its nose. For grooming, you'll need a kit consisting of a curry comb, comb for the mane and tail, a soft brush and a dandy (stiff) brush, a sweat scraper, a hoof pick, and several towels.

Since all horses aren't the same size and shape, these are points you must consider when shopping for tack. If you were lucky enough to get a saddle and bridle as part of the deal when you bought your horse, or even paid extra for them, the

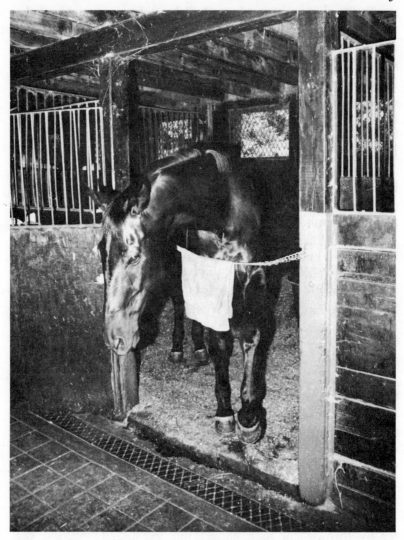

A chain or rope across the open stall door will keep a horse inside temporarily.

problem has already been solved. If not, before you shop for them, measure your horse's height and girth around the barrel. Also, note any irregularities in its conformation, such as a wide back or high withers. Sometimes you can find used tack at a local saddlery or school, and there's a good possibility it might fit your horse. Don't buy leather that is too worn or cracked, unless it's a part that's easily replaced.

Whether you buy used or new tack, have its fit on your horse checked as soon as possible by an experienced horseman so you can exchange it if necessary. The bit should be wide enough for the horse's mouth, and the bridle bands not too tight. The saddle should fit you as well as the horse, but shouldn't be so large that it presses against the withers. If you want an English or flat saddle, you'll find several varieties. The simplest is just a seat with stirrups for hacking. There's also a forward seat saddle with a raised cantle and knee pads designed especially for jumping. The third is the most common with a conventional seat that will carry you comfortably on all pleasure rides including occasional jumping; it probably is the type on which you took your riding lessons if you're an Easterner. Prices for fine Hartley English saddles start at $300, but a recent import from Argentina sells for as little as $100, complete with stirrups and fittings. You'll also need a felt or synthetic pad that is the same shape as the saddle and fits under it to protect the horse's back. It costs about $10. Since the Western or stock saddle is not as simple in design and is more ornate, it is more expensive, averaging $300. Instead of resting on a pad, it rests on a saddle blanket, which, like the pad, costs about $10. Prices for snaffle bridles start at $35. A bridle with a Pelham bit, requiring two pairs of reins, is more expensive. For specific information on tack and its prices, send for the catalogue issued by Eiser's, Inc., 1304 N. Broad Street, Hillside, New Jersey 07205. Or the *Saddlelog* from the Tex Ten Western Leather Co., Box 711 Yoakum, Texas 77995, which specializes in Western tack.

It's wise to buy the finest tack you can afford. It will fit your horse better and will last longer, saving you the expense of replacing it eventually. But how long it lasts will also depend on how well you take care of it. Like new boots which must be broken in to fit your feet, a new saddle will gradually adapt itself to the contour of your horse. To help the process, work a generous amount of neat's-foot oil into the leather, also into the leather bridle. This makes it more pliable as well as conditions it. Repeat after every use, also cleaning it first with saddle soap.

In your tack room, if you carelessly throw your saddle on the floor, it will eventually lose its shape. Improvise a saddle rack from a carpenter's sawhorse by adding a two-by-four on each side alongside the top to make it wider. An attractive wrought-iron rack with a wall bracket costs about $15 from Tex Tan. Many horsemen hang bridles and halters on wall hooks, but their weight can damage the leather where it bends sharply over the hook. A better way is to hang them on a short piece of two-by-four with its top rounded and one end nailed to the wall. Saddle blankets and pads also need kind treatment; they're usually damp after use and have to dry out. Hang them over a tight, short clothesline. The wind-up kind is handy for a tack room; when the line isn't being used, it can be rewound

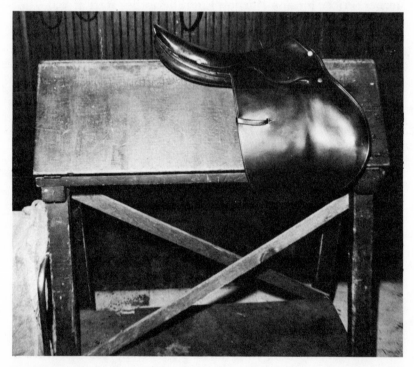

Buy a saddle rack or make one. A saddle tossed on the floor will soon lose its shape.

into its container.

Even if you have only a corral without a stable, you'll also need at least a paddock. A horse that is confined to a stall or small area and is exercised only when its rider takes it out is apt to become hard to handle, anxious, and often nervous. One acre is almost a minimum size for a paddock. It need not be a pasture covered with lush grass, although this would be an ad-

Wall racks for saddles can also be used for bridles which can be damaged if hung on thin metal hooks.

vantage, as would some shade trees and a running brook. What is important is that it be free of poisonous weeds and briars. If you desire, you can seed it with pasture grass of a type recommended by a feed supplier. The fence should be safe, strong, and high enough (at least 4 feet) so your horse won't be tempted to jump it. Split rails are nice but expensive. Board fencing can be just as serviceable if it is installed correctly. Posts should be no more than 8 feet apart, and the lowest board should not be less than 1½ feet above the ground. At the corners you can leave openings wide enough for you to walk through but too narrow for your horse. All wood should be treated with creosote.

An electric fence is practical and often the least expensive, and is not cruel. Its jolt won't injure your horse, only convince it that the world beyond the wire is off-limits. But hang cloth on the wire between the posts so the horse can locate it; while frolicking it might run right through it if it can't see it. Also put up signs warning neighbors not to touch the wire. And keep it clear of tall weeds, trees, and fallen branches that might ground it. An electric gate is seldom satisfactory; it's too flimsy. A gate made of boards is better. Hang it so it swings into the paddock; then your horse won't be able to force it open by shoving its weight against it. Sliding bars are often used instead of a gate, but some horses learn to push them aside. Yours may be one of them. Never use barbed wire in a fence, for obvious reasons.

If your pasture is large enough, divide it into two sections. Let your horse spend six months in one of them and an equal time in the other. This arrangement gives the section not being used time to grow and reseed itself. It also reduces the concentration of worms, present in every pasture and one of a horse's natural afflictions.

11. Keeping It Fit and Happy

For centuries, the horse grazed on wild grasses which apparently supplied enough nourishment; it survived without difficulty. Certainly the hard-working herds ridden by the Indians received nothing better, even on the Western plains where grass was scarce. Only when no pasture at all was available did horse owners have to provide substitutes. Logically, if your horse has a lush pasture of at least one acre, you shouldn't have to worry about extra feed for it. But maybe the pasture doesn't have a sufficient variety of grasses to supply all the needed nutrients; maybe it's in a part of the country where it won't stay green all winter. Then your horse's diet will be your responsibility at least some of the time, and year-round if it's confined to a stable. It's easy to tell if your horse is not getting the right feed or enough of it. It will begin to look thin and bedraggled, will lose the bloom on its coat and appear listless.

Almost as good as fresh grass is the dried grass we call hay; in a way it's similar to our own dehydrated foods. It contains the tops of selected grasses such as clover and timothy. Clover is richest in protein; timothy is mostly roughage. Sometimes alfalfa is added to hay as an aid to digestion, but it should be fed only occasionally and in small quantities if your horse isn't accustomed to it, otherwise it can *sour* the horse like a strong lax-

ative. But hay alone isn't sufficient. It is the nature of a horse
to graze almost continually, keeping its stomach almost full,
and it can't do the same in a stable. If forced to eat only hay
several times a day, it will be so hungry by its next meal that it
will over-eat and soon enlarge its stomach, like a man who
drinks too much beer and grows a beer belly. In a horse it's
called "hay belly," and it has the same result. Not only will
such a man or horse not win any beauty contests, but neither
will they do much running and jumping.

The solution is to feed with the hay a food concentrate, such
as grain, which will satisfy the horse's appetite at least temporarily. One of the most reliable grains is oats which contain
easily converted protein, vitamins, and minerals to provide energy and build muscle. Corn is almost pure carbohydrate, high
in calories for quick conversion into energy. These will be
burned off easily by an active horse but will soon add pounds
to one that doesn't get much exercise. This isn't always lamen-
table; your horse will appreciate some extra layers of fat during a severe winter.

Hay is measured by the ton which contains from 30 to 40
compressed bales, each measuring about 1½×1½×3 feet and
weighing between approximately 50 and 65 pounds. The price
varies between $50 and $100 a ton, depending not only on
demand but also on how well the grass grew that season. Break
open a bale and examine the hay before you buy it. A certain
amount of dust is unavoidable, but shop elsewhere if there
seems to be too much; you're paying for hay, not dust. The hay
should be slightly green and smell fresh. If it's too green and
moist, it's probably undercured and will finish its curing process in your storage shed where it might generate enough heat
to cause spontaneous combustion or, at least, give your horse
colic. If it's too brown, it is probably overcured and practically
worthless as food. Don't settle for hay that contains too many
weeds or shows signs of mold or that it has been a playhouse
for rats.

Grain comes in sacks priced from $50 to $100 each, depending largely upon how close you are to the source of supply.
Mixtures are available, such as oats and corn, but it's easier to
control your horse's diet if you buy both separately and mix

your own. Soybean meal and bran can be added to each feeding, also vitamin supplements especially if your horse is aged.
Your vet will advise you concerning these. Some mixtures are
know as *sweet feeds;* these contain ingredients such as molas-
ses which will help your horse's appetite if this becomes a
problem. You've surely read science-fiction stories that tell how
someday we'll be able to swallow a pill for a complete meal
instead of wrestling with a full plate of steak and mashed po-
tatoes. That day is already here for your horse. There are all-
in-one pellets which contain all the nutrients of hay and oats
including minerals, vitamins, etc. Their disadvantage when fed
exclusively, as it might also be for us, is that they aren't very
soul-satisfying, nor do they provide roughage. But they are
handy on a trail ride or camping trip because they're easy to
carry. They can also be added to your horse's regular feed to
make up for deficiencies.

You will have to determine how much to feed and how often
by trial and error because every horse has a different metabo-
lism. Remember it is the natural instinct of a horse to eat con-
stantly, a small amount at a time. If you give it an unlimited
supply at one meal, it will eat until it's sick and this can be serious because, unlike your family dog or cat, it can't vomit.
Probably the best feeding schedule for the horse, but not for
you because it would take up all your time, would be to feed it
small quantities all day long. As a compromise, the general
rule is to decide on the number of feedings according to how
hard your horse works. If it works very hard every day, it will
need three or even four. If it's permitted little or no exercise,
this can be reduced to two.

The amount of grain fed at each meal depends not only on
the horse's activity, but also on its size. Obviously a large horse
needs more than a pony. A 1,000-pound, active horse needs at
least 10 quarts of grain divided into its three feeds. If it rests
periodically during the day, this can be reduced to 8 quarts
split into two feeds, and 5 quarts into two feeds if it stands in
its stall most of the time. Less is required for smaller horses. A
small pony may be satisfied with no more than two quarts
daily. Realize that these amounts are only approximate. Increase them if your horse gets too lean; decrease them (or

eliminate some of the corn) if it gets too fat.

Your horse also needs salt. The best way to provide it is to hang a salt block in its stall so it can take as much as it needs. And it must have plenty of fresh, clean water, which should always be available. If it isn't, never feed your horse until it has been watered. With water in its stall, it will instinctively drink first. Then feed the hay, finally the grain. Meal times are negotiable. They needn't be exactly at sunrise, noon, and sunset. Choose the hours most convenient to you, but once you have set a schedule, your horse will be happier if you stick to it. It will also prefer to be served each meal at the same place.

As necessary as nutritious feed to your horse's good health and condition is cleanliness, and it begins in the stall. For bedding, cover the floor with a generous layer of straw or sawdust. It should be cleaned daily. Tie your horse outside, rake out all the straw and let the clay floor dry thoroughly. Then mix with a fresh supply the straw that hasn't been soiled, and recover the floor. If you are using sawdust, remove the soiled portion, turn over the remaining wet spots so they can dry, then add more till the floor is covered. Don't allow manure from the stall to accumulate near the stable. The biting flies that have tortured horses since *Eohippus* breed in it, as do all kinds of bacteria and worms. Until you can sell it to a neighbor as fertilizer (it's especially good for growing mushrooms), or use it in your own garden, or dispose of it at the village dump, store it in some remote pit where its aroma won't offend neighbors who aren't as fond of horses as you are. For a solitary horse, large plastic garbage bags offer one solution. Don't pile it out in the pasture or a similar place that's easily accessible. For a reason that still baffles animal behaviorists, the most sophisticated house cats and dogs, and even purebred horses themselves, take a fiendish delight in rolling in it, especially when it's fresh.

Some horsemen claim that to a horse a good grooming is worth a bushel of oats. This may be an exaggeration. Wild horses are happy and healthy, and they've never seen a curry comb. But at least it will make your horse look and smell better. It might also stimulate the skin and hair growth. A horse doesn't need a shampoo; the natural oils of its skin and hair

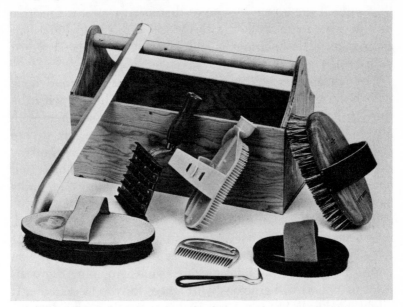

Grooming keeps your horse clean and its coat in good condition. Note the hoof pick in this grooming kit.

will shed dirt, but they'll do it faster with your help. And all of us like massage whether we need it or not. A touch-up grooming of your horse before you ride it will keep you cleaner, too. The time for a thorough grooming is after vigorous exercise.

If you and the horse are still comparative strangers, introduce it to your grooming ritual with some diplomacy. While it's crosstied, talk to it, show it a brush, give it a few strokes on the neck. Eventually it will learn to recognize your intention and will look forward to being groomed. First use the curry comb; a rubber one is less irritating to the skin than one of metal. Start with the neck, and work over the chest between the forelegs, the outside of the top forelegs, the body, the outside of the top hind legs, then the hindquarters, using a circular motion. This will loosen the dirt and dead hair. Don't skip the area under the tail. Clean the comb when it becomes clogged. Next use the dandy (stiff) brush with short lifting strokes in the direction in which the hair grows; this removes the loosened dirt and hair. Use it also on the horse's face and the inside of the upper legs, areas that usually are too sensitive for the curry comb. Follow with the soft brush to give the hair a sheen, and as a final touch, "polish" away the remaining dust with a soft cloth.

The lower parts of the legs are mostly just skin and bone with little or no flesh. These can be brushed lightly with the soft brush. If they're covered with caked mud, soak them with a wet cloth. Next comb the mane and tail, using short strokes and untangling any snarls with your fingers, not by yanking the comb which will only pull out the hairs. If you should pull out some mane or tail, the horse won't complain; their roots have no nerve connections.

Finally, with a hoof pick, remove any dirt or pebbles which might have become wedged in the hollows of the hooves. At the same time check for loose shoes or injured frogs. If you desire, you can do the hoof picking before grooming the coat. A trained horse will graciously lift a hoof for you to examine. It might need a slight persuasion, such as a gentle push sideways; then when it lifts the hoof to move, you can grab it. If it re-

The triangular pad in the sole of the hoof is the frog. The pick is used to clean out the crevices along its sides and in its center.

fuses to co-operate, get your blacksmith to show you how it's done. Then, the first time you do the same successfully, give your horse a bribe such as a lump of sugar or a carrot. It's the better part of the pleasure/pain teaching system discussed in a previous chapter. The only trouble with bribing is that eventually your horse will lift a hoof every time it sees you, but then you can explain to friends that you've taught it to shake hands.

In summer, you'll also use a sweat scraper. A hot, sweating

horse cools off slowly, but you can help by giving it a shower with plenty of warm water to which some coat conditioner has been added. Then scrape it gently everywhere except the lower legs, and afterward dry it with towels, including the legs. If it's sweating from hard work, however, toweling isn't enough. Like an overheated car engine, you must let it idle for a time to help it cool off. Walk it until it's completely dry, except the legs, to keep the blood circulating. Otherwise it might founder, an ailment we'll discuss later.

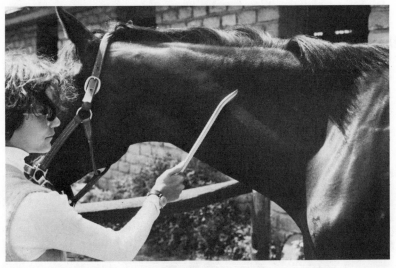

When your horse sweats from either hot weather or hard work, it's time to use the sweat scraper.

In summer, too, the biting flies are more numerous and horses with tender skin suffer the most. Sometimes it's best to keep them in their stalls instead of a pasture so you can ease their grief with a good insect repellent. In winter your horse needs more fuel to keep warm, so increase its feed. And if you're going to do much cold-weather riding, you'll have to clip off some of its heavier winter coat so that when it's worked hard, it won't get too hot. But it will miss this insulation when it's just resting in its stall during cold weather. Compensate for the loss of its natural coat by providing it with a blanket.

Add a heavy sheet if the cold is severe.

One of the indispensable items you must have in order to handle your horse in the stable and paddock is the halter with which you can lead it and hold it. It's a head harness, simpler than a bridle and easy to put on when your horse returns from its free time in the pasture. It shouldn't be worn in the pasture, however, because it might catch in some obstruction, be too strong to break, and your horse might injure itself struggling to get loose. Made of rope or leather straps, it consists of a nose band and crown joined by three straps, one along each cheek and the third under the chin. To put it on your horse, stand at the near shoulder with your left arm through the nose band to hold the halter within easy reach, and lay the rope or leather lead, which has been snapped beneath the chin band, across the withers. To steady the horse, hold its nose with your left hand and the mane with your right hand. Then quickly pull up the halter with your right hand so the horse's nose slips

A halter is a stable necessity for holding or leading your horse, also for tying it outdoors.

through the nose band, and buckle the crown strap behind its ears.

When you tie your horse, tie it by the halter, never by the bridle reins if you can possibly avoid doing so, especially if you have to leave it for more than a couple of minutes. If your horse is tied by its bridle and panics for some unforeseen reason, the bit is likely to injure the mouth. In Western movies the cowboys casually tie their reins to a hitching rail and spend all day in a local saloon. Either their horses never get bored, are panic-proof, or have mouths of steel. The real answer is that they're well-trained movie horses.

Tie your haltered horse to a solid object such as a fence post or tree, not to a loose rail or fence board. The position of the tie should be as nearly as possible on a level with the withers; too high such as on an overhead tree limb, or too low such as on your car's bumper, will pull the head at an unnatural angle and tempt the horse to fight it. In the latter case, you'll also get a few extra dents in your car. A rope that's too long invites disaster; the horse might entangle one of its legs in it or even manage to put a noose around its neck. One that's too tight is as bad. It is a horse's instinct to fight to free itself from any confinement with which it isn't familiar, and it usually will keep trying to escape until it hurts itself, often severely.

The halter is also used to hold your horse during *lungeing* (soft "g" as in "sponge") which is a method of exercising it without riding it. It consists of having the horse walk and trot in a circle at the end of a 25-foot rope, one end of which is snapped to a ring on its halter or on a *cavesson* (special nose band) while you stand in the center of the circle holding the other end. For this you will also require a long whip or a reasonable facsimile, not for punishing your horse or to frighten it, but only as a long-distance aid. An old fishing rod with a length of heavy cord tied to its tip can serve as well, but don't cast the cord overhand; the horse might think you really are going to strike it. With either a real whip or a homemade version just flick the end behind the horse or against its hind legs to start it walking, to speed up the walk, and to cause it to trot. Flick it in front to make the horse slow or stop. Don't try a gallop; not only might you lose your grip on the rope but you might become a bit dizzy since you have to keep turning to keep up with the horse. A lungeing workout of 45 minutes should provide sufficient daily exercise. And it shouldn't be a difficult chore; if your horse has had any training at all, it will be familiar with the routine.

The horse on which you've been taking riding lessons or rented from a riding academy has always been tacked up for you, ready to go. But now you must do it yourself. When you've watched how quickly and expertly your instructor dressed your horse, it seemed easy. The first few times you try it, you'll probably change your mind. It involves a few tricks you might not have noticed.

The horse is tied by its halter and you bring out the bridle, saddle, and saddle pad (blanket if it's a Western saddle). If you're going to put on the bridle first (the order isn't important but many horsemen prefer to put on the saddle last), rest the saddle and pad over the door of the stall or some other convenient object. If you have to leave the saddle on the ground, stand it upright on its pommel, the pad on top. While holding the bridle's crown strap in your left hand, with your right hand slip the reins over the horse's head. Next unbuckle and remove the halter with your right hand; you can hold the horse by the reins if it's tempted to move away. Lift the crown strap to its head, and press the head down, also using your right hand on its nose if you need some help. Then with your right hand under the chin, squeeze your fingers into the back corners of its mouth and the mouth will open. Quickly lift the bridle by its crown and guide the bit between the jaws so it rests over the tongue on the bars. This squeezing trick is well known to vets and pet owners; there's no other way to make a dog or cat open its mouth for a pill. And it involves no danger of being bitten, even with a horse, because at the corners of the jaws there are no teeth.

While you're guiding the bit, lift the crown to its position over the ears. Finally, fasten the throat latch, just tight enough so you can insert your flat hand beneath it. If any of the forelock is caught under the brow band, pull it free. Unbridling and replacing the halter is almost the same procedure in reverse. But don't yank on the bit to pull it out; you might hurt

To make a horse open its mouth for the bit, squeeze the rear of its jaws with your fingers. The plastic gadgets on this bridle keep the bit from slipping sideways.

the horse's mouth. The horse will spit it out with no argument. Some horses are more co-operative than others, of course. If you're having trouble, you might have to try bribing it as was suggested to make it lift a hoof. Then if it also opens its mouth for its bribe every time it sees you, you can say you taught it to smile, too.

Before putting on the saddle, it's best to have the stirrup irons run up on their straps, and the cinch completely un-buckled so it can't get in the way. This should have been done when you *tacked down* your horse (removed its tack). First examine your horse's back for sore spots and abrasions. Put on the pad and then center the saddle on top of it. Don't slam down the saddle; your horse might become annoyed. Place the saddle and pad farther forward than they should be, then you

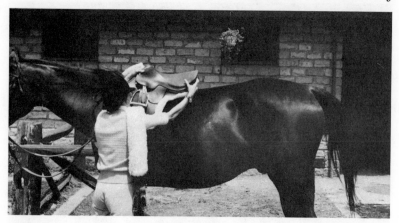

First put on the saddle pad, then gently lay—don't throw—the saddle on the pad. Finally attach the cinch.

can slide them back so the hair beneath them will be smoothed the right way. The correct position for the saddle is with its pommel just in back of the shoulder blades. Rock the saddle slightly and press down on it until it settles in place. Buckle on the cinch, tightening first one side then the other. It's tight enough when you can just pass your flat hand beneath it. But some horses have learned that if they puff out their bellies when the cinch is being tightened and deflate them afterward, they can relieve the tension. To outsmart them, after pulling down the stirrups and adjusting their length if necessary, before mounting check the cinch once more. As with the bridle, removing the saddle is the reverse of putting it on. Make sure the pad is kept clean. After every ride, it and the part of the horse's back it covers will usually be soaked with sweat. Wipe the horse's back with a towel and launder the pad.

The two most common ailments your horse can get are *colic* and *founder*. Colic is a stomach-ache, usually caused by overeating especially before a hard workout, by drinking too much when overheated, or by eating poor food which causes gas. Your horse will be restless, might try to bite its sides, or roll on the ground to relieve the pain. Severe cases may require a vet, but usually the horse recovers by itself if you take away its feed and water and keep it in the stall. Founder is an inflammation of the feet, usually the forefeet, and is caused by any condition that decreases blood circulation such as when an overheated horse drinks cold water or is given a cold shower; the body temperature drops and the heart doesn't pump hard enough to circulate blood through the feet. Another cause is overfeeding and underexercising; the blood concentrates in the digestive system, and the heart doesn't work hard enough to remove congested blood from the feet. The symptoms are hot and sore foot or feet, and the horse will become restless and show signs of lameness. In severe cases, a vet will have to lance the foot to let it drain. First aid is to increase blood circulation by making the horse walk which will be painful. Standing the horse in a cold pond or stream will ease the pain and also increase circulation. When we have sore feet, we raise them and rest them on a chair or desk; a horse can't do the same, but the next best thing is to make it lie down so the blood won't have to flow upward against gravity.

Two bacterial infections your horse might catch because they are very contagious, are *strangles* and *shipping fever*. The former is somewhat similar to mumps, even to the swelling under the jaw and difficulty in swallowing, accompanied by a running nose. But in a horse the swellings sometimes become abscessed and spread. Shipping fever is similar but not as serious; it is a variety of flu with most of the usual human symptoms. But both can result in pneumonia or worse and can be fatal if not treated quickly with large amounts of antibiotics. If your horse gets a running nose and pink eyes, call the vet as soon as possible. In a large stable containing a number of horses, if one gets shipping fever all of them must be administered antibiotics as a precaution. There is no natural immunity to this disease but there is to strangles; once a horse has recovered from it, it will never get it again.

If your horse's coat begins to look dull and drab, it's probably due to stomach worms; take a manure specimen to the vet to let him check it and administer the worming medication if necessary. In any case, it's a good precaution to have your horse wormed twice a year because these little parasites are abundant in every stable, paddock, and pasture and can't be

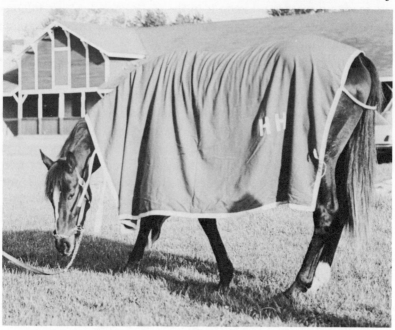

For chilly weather, especially in a stall, your horse will be more comfortable wearing a sheet or light blanket.

avoided. On these visits he can also check your horse's teeth, *floating* (filing down) any sharp points which might irritate its mouth. And on one of the visits he can give your horse a tetanus booster shot, necessary once a year. In fact, one of these boosters is advisable after any injury that cuts the skin, even a minor scratch. The cut itself, if not too deep, you can treat with a first-aid kit. If your horse is ridden outside the paddock, it should be shoed. Since its hooves keep growing, almost as fast as our own toenails, they should be trimmed every six weeks. This also entails removing the shoes and resetting them.

Your horse's temperature is usually a good indicator of its general health. About 100 degrees is normal; 102 or more means a fever. But when taking its temperature, use a large veterinary rectal thermometer. And be sure to tie a strong cord to it; otherwise you might lose it inside the horse!

SECTION IV
Riding for Ribbons

12.   On Woodland Trails

You don't have to confine your riding to a ring, paddock, or the local bridle paths. Take a trail ride, a cross-country trip through the great outdoors where you can camp in some wilderness forest, fish a wild mountain stream, and sleep under the stars like the old pioneers when the horse was the principal means of transportation. Today there are thousands of trails leading through our country's most scenic areas, and riding them is becoming one of the horseman's favorite sports. Not only for pleasure; many of the rides are competitive, the awards based on your horsemanship and the performance of your horse on the long trail. You can participate on pleasure trail rides even if you don't own a horse.

When the old-timer prepared to ride overland, he just tacked up old Betsy, strapped on his saddlebag, and took off, following a public trail. He often rode alone, hunted and fished for food, and solved unexpected problems when he came to them. Riding the trail today is not quite that simple. Woodland trails cross property that's either privately owned or under government control such as the State and National Parks and Forests. And since riding them is now a sport, not just a means of travel, each ride might have as many as a hundred horsemen. Adequate organization and supervision are neces-

A trail rider stops to rest and to view Arizona's Sycamore Canyon.
(U. S. Forest Service.)

sary to keep everyone—property owners and law enforcement officers—happy and contented.

The pleasure rides attract more horsemen than do those involving competition. They are social events, sometimes beginning with a get-acquainted party the night before and ending with a banquet after the ride. The riders set out at a leisurely pace, covering from ten to twenty-five miles a day, to enjoy each other's company, the fun of riding, and the opportunity to live outdoors. The trip can last for only a day or for more than a week, and since the horse isn't required to work hard, any type can be used. A ride may have as its destination a point a hundred miles away, the riders using the same trail or a different one on their return. Or it can stop at a base camp from which the riders move out on various short trails that radiate from the base like spokes on a wheel, then return each afternoon in time for a swim or a bit of fishing before the evening meal.

Organizing such a ride is more complicated than it might seem. The trail must be clearly marked in advance and any hazards eliminated or avoided—such as impassable fallen trees, old wire fences, chuck holes, hills that are too steep, or ground that is unsafe. Old logging roads, if convenient, are used as part of the trail. Campsites are located near fresh water, and often not far from a road when the "chuck wagon" is a modern station wagon. On some rides there are even complete stables at these stopover points. There must be a staff to do the cooking and panwashing. And if the horses must be tied to a picket line at night, someone must be on guard duty; horses are sociable animals, but sometimes the most docile gelding will suddenly feel offended and start a fight. Riding rules must be made and obeyed, such as no galloping, straying from the trail,

On pleasure trail rides the pace is slow, and you'll enjoy good company as well as picturesque scenery. (U. S. Forest Service.)

or ungentlemanly (or unladylike) conduct. During the ride, there must be a leader to set the pace and a drag rider at the rear to prevent straggling. Also someone who knows first aid for both man and horse. Commercial wranglers who conduct trail rides always have a doctor and a vet, or reasonable facsimiles, in attendance. My friend Dr. Norman Hill, a noted New York City orthopedic surgeon and enthusiastic horseman, spends his summer vacations trail riding for a well-known Wyoming wrangler; he doubles as an MD and a horse vet.

Almost all large riding clubs and 4-H clubs conduct pleasure trail rides. Some are restricted to members only, but most accept guests for a fee, as little as $10 for a one-day trip. If you wish to use your own horse, you must bring it by trailer, but usually you can rent a horse from a stable in the vicinity. Announcements of these rides are sent to local riding schools, horse shows, and riding clubs. They're also included in the "Coming Events" sections of local newspapers and in *Equestrian Trails* magazine, Box 2086, Toluca Station, North Hollywood, California 91602. Perhaps the best-known—recommended if you really want to ride away as far as possible from the rat race—are the pack trips sponsored by the Trail Riders of the Wilderness, a division of the American Forestry Association. Many are scheduled each year, winding through such rugged and picturesque areas as Yellowstone National Park, the Great Smoky Mountains, and the High Sierras. Each lasts from a week to ten days and is limited to thirty riders. The pace is never faster than a trot, and you need not be a horseman with vast experience. Bring only your outdoor clothing, bedroll, and any personal luxuries you feel will be essential. The wranglers provide everything else, even the horses. In fact, they will not let you use your own horse; they prefer their own which they know are safe, sound, and guaranteed not to make trouble. Current costs vary from about $250 for a short trip to $450 for a long one, but the rides are so popular that your application must be submitted as soon as possible after the schedule is released in January. It may be obtained by writing the Trail Riders of the Wilderness, American Forestry Association, 1319 18th Street, N.W., Washington, D.C. 20036.

A good trail horse for a pleasure trip should not only be

The route through Idaho's Sawtooth Wilderness Area is sometimes rocky but the wrangler's horses are sure-footed. (U. S. Forest Service.)

physically sound, comfortable to ride, and easy to handle, but should also have a generous amount of *savoir-faire*, the ability to adjust sensibly to new situations. It's no fun to ride a horse that thinks there's a monster lurking behind every large boulder or tree branch swaying in the wind. Or insists on leading the others, or walking alongside a buddy. Or doesn't pick its way carefully over rough ground in its anxiety to keep up with the herd. It should be willing to eat different feed and drink water that isn't served in its customary bucket. If spending the night in a strange place makes it feel insecure and it frets and whinnies for attention, it will not only make all the other horses nervous, but will keep the riders awake. These faults are most common in young horses and those that have had no experience in trail riding, and will usually cure themselves in time. If your horse shows any behavior that might annoy other riders, tie a red ribbon to its tail so they'll know it's having problems. If your horse is a chronic fighter, don't even attempt to take it on a trail ride; you'll make enemies for life.

There are two types of trail-riding contests: the Competitive Ride and the Endurance Ride. In both, you use your own horse because they are essentially tests not of your horsemanship but of your horse's soundness and condition at the completion of the ride. The Competitive Trail Ride is easier for your horse and is the most popular. The trail is either 40 miles to be covered in one day, or 100 miles to be covered in three days, both within daily time limits of 6½ or 7 hours, depending on the terrain (20 miles in 3 hours for the third day of the 100-mile ride). A daily variation of about 20 minutes from these limits is permitted. In other words, as in a sports car rally, if you ride too fast or too slow you lose points.

The horses start out individually at about 30-second intervals, the time of departure of each noted as will be its time of

An abandoned dirt road through Arkansas' Ozark National Forest becomes part of the trail for these riders. (U. S. Forest Service.)

arrival at the end of the trail. Away from the starting point, the riders can travel together for companionship if they so desire, but usually the spirit of competition keeps them scattered. The horses are observed carefully by a vet as they pass various checkpoints; any that show signs of lameness or fatigue are withdrawn from the ride for their own safety. If a horse's "way of going" (carriage and leg action) are to be considered in the contest, or if there will be incident awards for horsemanship, a judge will also watch the passing riders. One of these checkpoints will be at the top of a steep hill where the horse will be most likely to show any signs of weakness.

Since the health of the horses is so important, not only to the animals themselves but also to the selection of the winner, the vets and other judges work almost continuously. Before the ride, they examine each entrant thoroughly to be sure it's sound enough to complete the course with no chance of serious injury. At this time, the owner declares all its blemishes such as lumps, bruises, and interference marks on the legs, and these are recorded so later they won't be penalized for having occurred during the ride. When the horses start, they trot by the judges since this gait is most apt to reveal any lameness. Then the judges move to the various checkpoints in order, sometimes by car along a side road. During each evening of the first two days of the three-day ride, they again examine the horses to make sure they can safely continue. At least one hour after the ride has been completed, the horses receive their final and complete examination and the one in best condition is chosen champion.

The choice isn't easy because all the horses will have numerous bumps, scratches, bruises, and other signs of wear that must be evaluated, and there will be only a slight difference between a winner and a runner-up. Each fault must be checked against the list previously declared by the rider. A small bump might be penalized more points than an aggravated saddle sore but less than an interference mark on the inside of a pastern. Many rides consist of Open Heavyweight and Open Lightweight divisions, based on the total weight of the rider and tack; then two champions must be determined—even more if there are also Novice and Junior categories. Finally the judges must choose the winners in still other classes if they are included in the ride, such as horsemanship, best stable management during stopovers, and best trail horse.

The large clubs that conduct pleasure rides usually include one or several competitive rides every year. These are also announced in *Equestrian Trails* magazine mentioned previously. One of the oldest in the country is that held annually by the Green Mountain Horse Association of South Woodstock, Vermont, on a hundred-mile, three-day trail through the scenic Vermont mountains. It is attended regularly by horsemen from many states and is considered among the most enjoyable. Similar rides are held in North Carolina, Virginia, and Florida.

There are hundred-mile rides in many of the Western and Midwestern states, too, but these are Endurance Rides; the entire distance must be covered in twenty-four hours! Shorter trails of fifty miles have time limits of twelve hours. They are conducted in a manner similar to the Competitive Rides, but obviously, the stress on the horses is tremendous and unless they're in near-perfect condition, their chances of even finishing the course are slim. The judges, all of whom are vets, are not only extremely strict in examining the applicants but

For the sportsman-rider, there are streams seldom fished because they are too remote for most hikers. (U. S. Forest Service.)

watch them with great care during the ride to make sure they aren't being pushed beyond their capabilities. The time limit of twenty-four hours (twelve for fifty miles) is a maximum; there is no minimum. Therefore, the ride is really a race. Prizes are based on time and the horse's condition at the finish. The "first horse in" gets the racing trophy regardless of its condition. Of the first ten to finish the one in best condition is awarded the Top Ten prize. All horses completing the course within the time limit also receive awards. And sometimes there are prizes for the first horse of a certain breed.

Although almost any horse or pony, reasonably sound and sociable, can be used on a pleasure trail ride, the choice becomes more limited for the competitive rides, especially the endurance contests. Geldings and mares are the favorites because of their easy-going temperaments and their sure feet, but occasionally stallions do well in the hundred-mile Western races. The age should be at least five; this is a requirement on most rides of any type. The most popular breeds for competition are the Arabian and Morgan, sometimes the Thoroughbred if it doesn't have weakened legs from racing on a track. And when a Quarter Horse qualifies for an endurance race, it is hard to beat. Purebreds aren't always the winners. Often a well-built grade horse will win the top trophy.

For all competition, the conformation as well as the soundness of the horse is all-important. It needn't be a beauty-prize winner with a regal head, graceful neck, and trim figure. Beauty won't help it on a hundred-mile rugged trail, walking or trotting uphill and down, sometimes running for long periods at a full gallop in endurance races. It must have a large chest for adequate lung capacity, a strong and rather short back to make the rider's weight easier to carry on a long trip, long and powerful hips, well-muscled stifles and forearms. Its hooves must be wide enough to provide stability on rough ground. If you think your horse can perform in competition, after having a vet check it for soundness, ask the opinion of an experienced trail rider. If their reports are encouraging, your job has just begun. For a long ride, whether or not it's in competition, like an athlete your horse must first be conditioned physically to burn off excess fat and harden its muscles. It must be done gradually. Start about six weeks before the ride. Exercise it for a half-hour twice a day, and increase each period by a half-hour on succeeding weeks until it is working four hours a day. Use different trails or paths if available so your horse won't get bored, include hills, and after the second week ride all the gaits. Whenever it show signs of becoming tired, rest it for a few minutes. On these practice trips, join other riders if you can, so your horse will get used to company. The week before the scheduled ride should be one of complete rest to avoid overtraining.

There are a number of general rules to remember on a trail ride. Some will make you and your horse more comfortable, others are safety precautions, and still others are just plain good manners. An important one to follow is to walk your horse the first mile out to loosen its muscles, and the last mile in to cool it off gradually. On the trail, don't gallop past another rider; you might spook the other horse if it's a bit nervous. When ready to pass, it's polite to say "Passing, please" and then walk your horse. And never pass the trail leader if you value his or her friendship. Don't ride close behind the rider in front of you; not only will you risk having your horse kicked in the head, but it might step on the hind hoof of the other horse and loosen its shoe. If there's no drag rider and you're at the end of the line, be sure to close gates after you except when the leader found them open; maybe the property owner left them open so his cattle could pass through them. If you don't know, ask. And if you come across cattle, pass them quietly so you won't disturb them.

Use caution; if you have to cross a highway stop, look, and listen, then cross it at a right angle as quickly as possible. When you come to a stream, let your horse have a drink or two but not all it can hold. And if it stops in the middle and paws the water, move it out fast; it's getting ready to roll over and you'll get a dunking. If you know the trail will cross a very steep hill, be sure your horse will be wearing a breast strap to keep the saddle from slipping forward. Otherwise take time to dismount and tighten the cinch when you come to the hill, and loosen it again slightly after you've reached the bottom on the other side. Change your position in the saddle at intervals as you ride; it will not only ease the pressure points on your rump but also on the horse's back.

The rule about always mounting and dismounting on the horse's near side doesn't apply on a trail ride; use the uphill side even though it's the horse's off side. It's easier. When you arrive in camp, tie your horse but leave it saddled for about a half-hour to discourage bumps which might form on its back when the pressure of your weight is released too quickly. On a lunch stop you can tie it to the branch of a tree by its bridle if the branch is weak enough to bend when it pulls. But never tie it within hoof range of another horse, especially on a picket line in an overnight camp. If your horse is sweating from exertion when you arrive in camp and you give it all it can drink, it might get colic or even founder. Give it all it can eat, too, and it's almost sure to get sick. Let it cool off for at least a half-hour, then drink in small quantities, and afterward feed it sparingly. The evening meal should be the largest of the day. When you tie your horse, use a bowline knot that can be released quickly in an emergency. If a horse breaks away from the picket line and runs, don't chase it, either on foot or horseback. When it sees it isn't chased, it will stop running. It won't stray far from the herd, and you'll have time to entice it back with some goodies. Last but not least—DON'T LITTER!

13. In the Show Ring

Ever since man made the horse his friend, he has used it in competition as well as work. The Mongol on the fastest horse in battle was honored as the best warrior. The Moors raced each other on the desert. Alexander the Great's chariots later raced in the Grecian Olympic games and inspired the races made popular by the ancient Romans. And in Medieval England the success of a jousting contest depended as much on the horse as it did on the prowess of the knight on its back. Now we have flat and harness racing, polo, rodeos—and horse shows. Today's horse shows are open to any rider who desires to participate and believes "anything the other horses can do, mine can do better." They're enjoyed by everybody, spectators as well as riders and horse owners. And to a horseman there's no greater thrill than riding off with a blue ribbon or a trophy, not to mention the prize money that comes with it. But even if you don't win, it's still fun.

There are types to suit all competitors, varying in the number of events and lasting from one to three days. Most clubs and associations sponsoring them are members of the American Horse Shows Association (AHSA) which has established the rules for fair competition and rates the sponsors according to their facilities and the caliber of the horsemen who compete

During a show, concentrate on showing. Obviously, this American Saddle Horse is aware of its importance. She is Plainview's Julia, five-gaited world's grand champion. (American Saddle Horse Breeders Association.)

in them. Therefore, a blue ribbon from a B-rated show will count more on the AHSA records than one from a show rated C. The events at a show are classified in general divisions, each of which has a number of classes based on various factors such as the type of riding, the age and experience of both the riders and their horses, height of fences for hunters, sometimes on the horses' size.

These contests in an Eastern show are usually confined to riding the flat or English saddle and the divisions feature dressage, equitation, hunters, jumpers, and often simulated trail riding. Southern shows also have classes for the three- and five-

gaited saddle horses. In the West, the usual events are equitation, simulated or actual trail riding, pleasure riding, stock
horse with or without cattle, cutting, and roping. In a show
confined to a specific breed, there will be a halter or model
(beauty) class in which the horse isn't ridden but is shown on
a halter. Each show publishes a program called a prize list,
copies of which are sent to clubs and schools in the area. An-
nouncements of large regional and national shows can be
found in such magazines as the *Chronicle of the Horse,* Mid-
dleburg, Virginia. To understand the program and the qualifications necessary to enter the various classes, you must be familiar with show language. Realize that most contests are based
on the performance of the horses, not of their riders, although
it takes a good rider to make a horse perform at its best.

Dressage ("training" in French), one of the Eastern events,
is an evaluation of how well the horse has been trained to en-
hance its natural gaits in response to the rider's aids. For a national winner with near-perfect performance the aids might be
so slight that it seems the rider is using none at all. Equitation
is mainly a measure of the rider's ability. The shows make a
distinction between hunters and jumpers. Working Hunters
are judged on their walk, trot, canter, sometimes their hand
gallop, and on jumping fences rarely higher than 4 feet. The
winner is the one considered most desirable for an actual fox
hunt. A Green Working Hunter is a beginner that has had only
one or two years of competition in classes requiring jumping;
one-year horses are required to take lower fences about 3½
feet. Sometimes hunters are also classified according to the
weight they carry; a lightweight up to 165 pounds, middle-
weight from 165–85, and a heavyweight over 185 pounds.

In the judging of Conformation Hunters, a horse's appearance and breed points are also factors; a scar is penalized
whereas in a Working Hunter it would be simply a mark of
honor. Jumpers are judged entirely on their jumping ability
and style, regardless of their age, sex, or breed. They are
classified according to how much money they've won previously jumping at other registered shows. The Open Jumper
Class, one of the most common, is for horses that have won at
least $2,000. The fences are about 4 feet high but also spread

In large shows, there are classes requiring more formal attire. This is a student at Meredith Manor's "college" of horsemanship at Waverly, West Virginia. (Meredith Manor School of Horsemanship.)

up to 4 feet. One of the most exciting jumper classes, not only for the rider but also for the spectator, is the Puissance ("strength" in French); the fences are gradually increased in height, as well as spread, until they are higher than 7 feet.

A horse's show experience determines its qualifications for the Maiden, Novice, Limit, and Intermediate classes in AHSA

shows, but in unregistered shows these terms sometimes apply
to the riders. Technically a Maiden is a horse that has not yet
won a blue ribbon in a similar class at a registered show; a
Novice is one that has won less than three such ribbons; the
Limit Class is for a horse that has won less than six; and the
Intermediate for one that has won less than twelve. Some
classes are for the amateur riders only. You are an amateur
under all conditions until you reach the age of eighteen, and
you'll remain one thereafter even when you accept prize
money except in the equitation events; the reason is that in
equitation the money is awarded for *your* performance, not
your horse's. Usually the show protects you from temptation in
such cases by awarding only ribbons. But you are a professional, not an amateur, and you will face tougher competition
against other pro's in a show if you work, or have ever worked,
for a salary in a job involving horses, such as a riding instructor
or stable hand, even a part-time summer job. Or even if you
have worked free for a member of your family who is classified
as a pro, receiving an income from breeding, training, or stabling horses or operating a riding school. Once you are
branded a professional, perhaps only because of temporary
employment, you can regain your amateur standing if you
plead ignorance before the AHSA and promise that in the future, horses will only be your hobby, not your business. The
Olympic Committee, of course, will never forgive you.

The Owners' Classes are open to you if you are an amateur
and either you or your family owns the horse. Junior Classes
are for riders under eighteen, and are sometimes subdivided
into age groups, such as under eleven, eleven to fourteen, and
fourteen to eighteen. There are no sex restrictions, but if you
are a lady over eighteen there are Ladies' Classes offering similar competition. To follow show rules, you might have to re-
evaluate your horse's age. As explained in an earlier chapter, a
Thoroughbred's birthday is always January 1, not the actual
date on which it was foaled. For convenience, in shows this
has become the rule for all breeds. Your horse's age on January
1 will be its age for the remainder of the year. Under the list-
ing of divisions and classes in the show's advance program
there will be other pertinent information such as the entry fee

In dressage classes at a show, the horse's training is evaluated; in equitation classes, the rider's ability is most important.

for each division (usually eight or ten dollars for shows of average size) the number of ribbons to be awarded (up to six) and the accompanying prize money (fifty dollars or more with a blue ribbon, proportionately less for the others), special trophies or medals, number and height of fences for hunters, etc. On a typical program you'll find such statements as: *eight horses to gallop one way of the ring, no martingales, outside course* (hunter course outside the ring), *8 fences 2'6", extreme speed will be penalized.* On programs of Western shows you'll find listed two gaits that might mystify you if you're an Easterner; these are the jog and the lope. The former is a very fast walk that is almost a slow trot. Ordinarily it's a rough ride; the trick is to make your horse perform it smoothly. The lope is a very slow canter, a natural gait of a wild horse which it can keep up for hours without becoming tired. In a show the rider must keep the horse collected while loping so the gait will be precise and under control.

At the show another program, called a catalogue, is issued for sale principally to the spectators. It is similar to the early prize list but also contains the names of all the committee members, officials and judges, and information on the horses and riders. One class entry might read: *"Bay Rum," D-G-5-15.* It means the horse's AHSA registered name is Bay Rum, and it's a dun-colored gelding, five years old, with a height of fifteen hands. This will be followed by the name of the owner, then the name of the rider if different. Beside providing the spectators with "the names and numbers of all the players," these programs are a source of substantial revenue to the show's sponsor. Over half the pages are often advertising. At benefit shows intended to raise money for a worthy charity, they can be almost as thick as local telephone directories, and even contain color ads.

Judges are selected by the sponsoring club or association from a long list of those registered with the AHSA, and they are paid a daily fee and expenses. At least two are required because not only might two rings be operating at the same time, but also a judge is seldom qualified to evaluate all types of competition. He or she might specialize in hunters, or dressage. At every registered show there is also a Steward who represents the AHSA and is paid by the sponsor. He is a supervisor who makes sure everything conforms to the AHSA rules all winning horses to enforce the AHSA's prohibition of the use and standards, that the show is run smoothly and fairly. He might also be required to check the credentials of the entrants. With the help of a vet, he has tests made of urine samples from of drugs. This service will cost you an extra dollar or two when you enter the show, even if your horse isn't a winner. At one

This Junior Hunter is judged on its walk, trot, canter, and on jumping fences, usually low.

time it was common practice to give a drooping horse a pep pill to make it more spirited, and a tranquilizer to calm one that had too much fire. Now such practice results in fines up to $1,000. A vet's job is an important one, and at a large show he has a staff of assistants. He must be available in emergencies, and administer first aid when necessary. If a judge thinks your horse isn't sound enough to compete, the vet makes the final decision, and if he agrees with the judge he will certify your withdrawal so you can recover your entry fees. He also makes private "stall calls," if you think your horse is ailing. And each show has its official photographer who is permitted to enter the ring with his camera to take action pictures of you and your horse, also a picture of you when you are awarded a ribbon—black-and-white photos cost from five to ten dollars each, from twenty-five to fifty dollars for one in color. Sometimes a large show will also have a tack supplier who sells everything from saddles to cinches in case you'd like to splurge, as winners frequently do, or if you find you've left some necessary

item at home. He makes repairs, too. And there's an official farrier in case your horse has shoe trouble.

You'll have to trailer your horse to the show. This means you
have to buy, rent, or borrow a trailer. If you keep your horse at
a boarding stable or riding school, the manager probably has
one you can rent—maybe a van for several horses so you can
invite other owners to enter the show and share the transportation. For long distances there are reliable horse shippers
with special vans, but they're expensive. If you have a winner
and intend to enter many shows, better buy a trailer and write
off the investment with your prize money. The wider two-
horse kind is preferred even though you have only one horse:
it provides room for your tack trunk, hay and grain besides
other essentials. Its loading ramp should have wings so the
horse won't see the ground and will feel more secure when it's
climbing it, and tie the horse by its halter to the front. There
should be at least a half-door in the rear so it won't fall out.
Before loading it, wrap its legs and ankles with special reusa-
ble bandages designed especially to protect them from hard
knocks en route. If the weather is variable, bring a sheet or
blanket to use when needed so the horse won't catch a cold.

A few days before you leave, make a list of everything you
must bring. You'll find you'll be adding to it daily. Don't forget
your rain gear and a good supply of grooming equipment for
yourself as well as for the horse; you're going to a *show*, not on
a camping trip. Be sure to include your regulation show outfit
of helmet, boots, gloves, and jacket, which the judge might let
you remove if the weather is too hot. If this seems likely, be
prepared to wear under the jacket a handsome, lightweight
vest over your subdued riding shirt. And don't forget a tie,
even if it's just the clip-on kind.

If there's one ailment to which your horse will be most sus-
ceptible, it is colic due to a change of water, and perhaps to
feed if it's suddenly subjected to a different diet, so bring your
favorite colic cure, one you know from past experience will
work. It might even be better than that supplied by the show
vet who doesn't know your horse as well as you do.

When you arrive at the show, unload your horse as soon as
possible and walk it around to loosen its muscles. If it's going

*Bathing and grooming before the show helps to qualify for a ribbon.
The horse must look its best.*

to be kept in a stall, inspect the accommodations first to make
sure they're safe and adequate. Just before the show, give your
horse a thorough grooming and don't forget to use the hoof
pick. There'll usually be a warm-up area near the ring; use it
for an hour until it's time for your event. Then report promptly
to the starter at the ring entrance gate, and he or she will tell
you your place in the line-up. Remember your number and
enter promptly when it is called. After you've completed the
course, leave the ring by the exit gate and return to the warm-
up area. You might be called back for a ribbon. If you are, it
might be pinned to your horse's bridle by a youngster or a little old lady, neither of whom know much about horses. Better
reach out and intercept the ribbon if you suspect your horse
might object to such strange goings on. If your horse is a winner and seems to be having an unusually fine day, the officials
might permit you to post-enter it in another event for which it
hasn't been previously scheduled. Most often they won't; it
complicates the bookkeeping. But some do, and there's no
harm in asking. When your horse is finished for the day, clean
it and cool it, water and feed it just enough to reward it for

doing its best. And make it comfortable in its stall if you're
going to stay overnight, which you certainly will if you've
amassed a pile of ribbons or one of the grand trophies or
medals; you won't want to miss the celebration at the evening
banquet.

Unless you are a professional and the success of your horse
or horses is important to your income, you'll be wise not to
take shows too seriously. Realize that they aren't the ultimate
test of your riding potential or your horse's performance. Accept a ribbon if you win one, as a bonus to your day of fun.
You've met other riders, made new friends, and you can improve your horsemanship by recognizing your mistakes. If you
can corner the judge, he might be persuaded to tell you your
faults, but don't approach him as a sore loser and don't argue.
His decisions are final and there's no way you can change
them. If you think he's been unfair, which he might have been,

*A Working Hunter is one you'd like to take on a real fox hunt.
Show classes provide outside courses with natural-looking barriers.*
(Robert Brummet from Meredith Manor School of Horsemanship.)

don't tell him so; just forget it. The AHSA rules are fair and explicit, but in all events except some of the jumping classes that are decided by a stop watch or faults at a fence, the results are a matter of opinion—his. You really can't blame him if he subconsciously prefers a Morgan to a Paint or places more value on a trot than a canter. Maybe he himself owns a Morgan that trots like a champion, and it is the standard to which he compares all others. It's a fact that in Western shows most judges favor the Quarter Horse. A judge will never deliberately be unfair, but his decisions are based largely on his own experiences, and in many cases these can influence his thinking. If you go to many shows and often see the same judge officiating, and if you don't mind expending a little extra effort, study his selections until you know his likes and dislikes. Then when you are scheduled to ride in one of his classes, you can prepare to give him what he prefers.

Remember that at a show you are *showing* yourself and your horse. Not only appearance and performance are important but also your showmanship. Even if you're not an expert or you're unsure of your horse, try not to reveal it to the judge. Don't be self-conscious, have the jitters, scowl, shake your head in disappointment, or squirm around in the saddle. Create the impression that you have everything under perfect control, and that you have complete confidence in your horse. Relax and make everything look easy, even if it isn't. Think positive. If you have any doubt that you're going to win a ribbon, you're a loser even before you climb into the saddle, so in the ring always act as if you expect one. By your attitude as you ride through the course, make the judge aware that if he doesn't think you deserve one, he needs better glasses.

Glossary

aged A horse at least nine years old.

aids The signals a rider uses in directing a horse: the reins, his knees, heels, body weight, voice, etc.

arm The upper foreleg reaching to the chest.

barrel The horse's body between the shoulders and hips.

bars Parts of the lower jaw, between the incisors and molars, on which the bit rests.

billets Saddle straps to which the cinch fastens.

bit The device, usually a metal bar, held in the horse's mouth and to which the reins are fastened for control.

blaze A large white patch on a horse's forehead, sometimes extending to the nose.

box stall A large stall, usually square.

breast plate Part of a harness; the strap across a horse's chest to keep the saddle from slipping backward.

bridle The head harness that holds the bit in position.

cannon The bone between the knee, or hock, and the fetlock.

canter One of the gaits; a slow gallop.

cantle The higher rear part of a saddle.

cinch A strap passing under the horse's barrel to hold the saddle in position.

collection The use of knee pressure and rein tension to make the horse more physically alert and to improve its balance.

conformation The parts of a horse and how they're assembled.

coronet   The part of the leg just above the hoof.

crop   A short riding stick carried by stylish horsemen.

crossbred   Having parents of different breeds.

croup   Back of a horse above the hips.

crown   Part of a bridle; a strap lying across the head behind the ears.

curb   A more severe bit than a snaffle for more positive control.

curry comb   A type of brush with metal or rubber teeth for removing loose hair and dirt from a horse's coat.

dandy brush   A stiff bristle brush for grooming.

diagonal   The diagonal pairs of hooves a horse uses in trotting.

dock   The root of the tail.

elbow   Upper joint of the foreleg.

equitation   A fancy word for riding a horse.

fetlock   The joint connecting the cannon and the pastern.

filly   A female horse less than three years old.

flank   The side of a horse's barrel.

flat saddle   Light, simple English type carrying the rider farther forward than does the Western saddle.

float   To file off the sharp edges of a horse's teeth.

forelock   A horse's bangs that hang forward between the ears.

forward seat   A rider's position close to the horse's withers.

founder   Inflammation of the feet caused by improper circulation.

frog   A soft triangular pad on the bottom of the hoof.

gait   The way a horse moves its feet as in the trot, canter, and gallop.

gallop   A horse's fastest gait.

gelding   A stallion that has been castrated.

girth   Same as *cinch;* also the circumference of the horse's body measured behind the withers.

grade   A crossbred horse.

hackamore   A bridle without a bit.

hand   Unit of measurement of a horse's height; one hand equals four inches.

hock   The lower joint of the hind leg.

hoof pick   Tool used to clean out crevices bordering the frog of a hoof.

irons   English term for stirrups.

jodhpurs   Tight-fitting riding pants extending to the ankles.

knee   Lower joint of the foreleg.

lead   The foreleg (right or left) that strikes the ground first during a canter or gallop.

lope   A slow Western canter.

lungeing   Exercising a riderless horse at the end of a long rope.

mare   A female horse over three years old.

martingale (standing)   A strap connecting the bridle and cinch to keep a horse from star gazing.

martingale (running)   A strap from the cinch, splitting into a Y across the horse's chest, each rein passing through a ring at the end of the Y.

muck out   To clean out a stall.

near side   The left side of a horse.

neck rein   To signal a horse by pressing a rein against its neck.

nose band   A bridle band encircling the horse's nose.

off side   The right side of a horse.

Pelham   A bit that combines a curb and a snaffle, requiring two sets of reins.

poll   The top of a horse's head.

pommel   The front raised part of a saddle.

post   To rise from the saddle during a recurring diagonal in a trot.

seat   Posture and position of a rider in the saddle.

shoulder   The place where the top of the foreleg joins the body.

snaffle   The simplest bit, a solid or jointed bar of metal or rubber.

snip   A white mark on a horse's nose.

sound   In good health and condition.

star   A white patch on a horse's forehead.

stock saddle   A deep Western saddle with a high pommel topped by a horn.

stripe   A very thin white line from forehead to nose.

tack   A horse's riding outfit of saddle and bridle; also a halter and other accessories.

throat latch   A bridle band that extends under the horse's neck to keep the bridle in place.

thrush   An inflammation of the frog.

tree   The wooden frame of a saddle.

trot   A gait in which a horse moves its legs in alternate pairs.

way of going   The style, body-carriage, and trail sense of a horse.

withers   The highest point of a horse's back above the shoulders.

INDEX

Affection, horse's temperament and, 45, 47, 120. *See also* Friendliness
Africa, horses in, 12, 64
Age of horse: aged, defined, 29, 168; competition and, 153, 160; teeth as indication of, 32; terms for, 28–29
Aids, control, 168; for cantering (galloping), 82–84, 85, 87; for changing leads, 87; defined, 168; fast gaits and, 77, 80, 81, 82, 83–84, 85, 87; for jumping, 90; leg (knee) and pressure points and, 66, 83; shows and, 152; walking and, 68–73, 74
Ailments, 140–42 (*see also* specific kinds); buying (choosing) a horse and, 112–13; most common, 140–42; shows and, 164
Alaska-Siberia land bridge, 5–6
Albino horses, 35
Alexander the Great, 8, 10, 11, 156
Alfalfa, in diet, 129–30
American Forestry Association, and pack trips, 148
American Horse Shows Association (AHSA), 42, 156–57, 159–60, 162–63
American Saddle Horse. *See* Saddle Horse, American
Antibiotics, use of, 141
Apache Indians, 18, 19
Appaloosa (breed), 20, 21, 40; described, colors, 20, 40
Approach: jumping, 90–93; to a strange horse, 53–54
Arabian horses (breed), 7–10, 12, 13, 15; and competition, 153; described, 36
Arm, 30, 168
Armor, 13, 19
Asia, horses in, 6, 8
Asphalt stall floors, 117
Attila the Hun, 11
Auctions, horse, 105
Ayllon, Vasquez de, 16
Aztec people, 16

Backing up, 70–71, 72
Bacterial infections, 141. *See also* specific kinds
Balaclava (horse), 8
Balance (*see also* Seat): in backing up, 70–71; in cantering

(galloping), 85; collection and, 69, 168; in jumping, 89–90, 91, 93, 95, 99; in walking, 69–70, 74–76
Bald face, 35
Bald Spirit (horse), 35
Barbs (breed), 12, 13
Bareback riding, 75
Barns, use as stables of, 119
Barrel, horse's, 30; defined, 168
Barriers, jumping, 89–99; approach, 90–93; bars, 92, 96–97; cavaletti, 97; extended (spread), 93; increasing height, 97; reins and, 95–96; speed and, 92–93, 96
Bars, barrier, 92, 96–97
Bars, horse's: hoof, 34; mouth, 32, 168
Bars, stirrup, 61–62
Bays, 35
Bearing rein, 70
Bedding, stall, 123, 132
Belgian (breed), 13
Bell mare, 29
Berber tribesmen, 12
Billets, 61, 168
Biting flies, 132, 135
Bits, 57–60, 168 (*see also* specific kinds); buying and cost, 125; defined, 168; first use of, 11; inserting, 138, 139; kinds, 57–60
Black horse, 35
Blankets: saddle (*see* Saddle blankets); stable, 123, 135–36, 142; for warmth, 123, 135–36, 142
Blaze marking, 34, 168
Blood bays, 35
Blood circulation ailments, 141. *See also* specific kinds
Blue roan, 36
Boarding stables, 115–17; choosing, 116; cleanliness and, 117; rates, 115–16; "rough board," 116; stalls and floors and, 116–17
Body position. *See* Seat
Boots, riding, 56
Bowed tendon, 113
Bowlegs, 110
Box stalls, 116, 119, 168
Bran, in diet, 131
Breastplate, 62, 168
Breeches, riding, 55, 56, 169
Bribery (bribing the horse), 134, 139 (*see also* Pleasure/pain

GIL PAUST was born in New York State but spent his early childhood on a New Jersey farm where, when he was eight years old, the family horse, Nell, was scared by a train locomotive and took him on an unscheduled ride cross-country. It was the beginning of his long association with horses, more pleasant than his first experience. Since then they have been his companions on many outdoor trips. One trip he considers most memorable was a recent climb through the Carpathian Mountains of Romania on a HUZUL, a breed indigenous to that country.

Mr. Paust has B.A. and M.A. degrees from Columbia University, has taught in high school and college. Then, as an aircraft pilot, he became an instructor of Air Force cadets. Later he joined the staff of a national magazine. He has had hundreds of his own stories published in addition to a dozen books. Until several years ago he was editor-in-chief of a national magazine with a circulation of over one million. In case you're interested, his favorite horses are the MORGAN, QUARTER HORSE, and the fantastic TENNESSEE WALKER.